The Ask Leo Guide to Staying Safe on the Internet

EXPANDED Edition

5th Edition

by

Leo A. Notenboom

https://askleo.com

ISBN: 978-1-937018-59-7 (PDF)
ISBN: 978-1-937018-60-3 (ebook)
ISBN: 978-1-937018-61-0 (paperback)

5.01

Table of Contents

The Ask Leo! Manifesto

I believe personal technology is essential to humanity's future.

It has amazing potential to empower individuals,
but it can also frustrate and intimidate.

I want to make technology work for you.

I want to replace that *frustration* and *intimidation*
with the *amazement* and *wonder* that I feel every day.

I want it to be a *resource* rather than a *roadblock*;
a *valuable tool,* instead of a source of *irritation*.

I want personal technology to empower you,
so you can be a part of that amazing future.

That's why *Ask Leo!* exists.

Leo A. Notenboom
<https://askleo.com>

First: A Freebie for You

You're looking at the EXPANDED version of my Internet Safety ebook, and I hope it's useful to you.

But before we dive in, I have something more for you: my *Ask Leo!* special report, ***10 Reasons Your Computer is Slow (and what to do about it)***. This report will help you identify why your computer is slowing down, and the steps you can take to fix it.

It's yours free when you register *this* book.

In fact, you'll also receive several additional free bonuses.
• The FREE version of *The Ask Leo! Guide to Staying Safe on the Internet*. A shorter, more compact version of this book that you can share with your friends and family.

- All available digital formats of the book as direct downloads. Regardless of which version you have, you can enjoy this book on the digital device of your choice.
- Digital updates for life.
- Errata and prioritized Q&A.

You'll find the information you need to register in a chapter near the end of the book. Once you register, you'll be taken to a web page that lists all available bonuses.

Be Sure to Register Your Book!

Your purchase of this book entitles you to several additional free bonuses.

- All available digital formats of the book as direct downloads. Regardless of which version you purchase, you can enjoy this book on the digital device of your choice.
- Digital updates for life.
- Errata and prioritized Q&A.

You'll find the information you need to register in a chapter near the end of the book. Once you register, you'll be taken to a webpage that lists all available bonuses.

Part 1: Protect Yourself

It Pays to Be Skeptical

A message pops up on your computer, warning you that malware has been detected.

What do you do?

The answer's not as clear as you might think.

In fact, no matter what you choose to do, it could be the wrong thing.

Your trust is a commodity

It's no secret that scammers actively prey on the trusting.

But it's not just scam artists who abuse our generally good nature and desire to trust. Hackers, malware authors, overly-aggressive salespeople—essentially anyone who wants something— re skilled at using your trust against your better interests.

Consider that warning message that popped up...

Warning: malware detected, click to remove ...

A pop-up message telling you there's malware on your machine (and click here to fix it) is probably no big surprise to most people. With the constant barrage of news reports about hacks and malware and the ongoing emphasis on anti-malware tools, your first response on reading such a message may be to believe it.

"Malware? Well, it happens to so many people, it's no surprise that it happened to me!"

Except ... it might not have.

Not yet, anyway.

That message might be completely fake. It may be inciting you to trust it and click to take further action. And that click and "further action" could install malware, or worse.

Or it could be legitimate.

What do you do?

Unable to deliver package, details attached...

You've probably received email—important-looking email—that indicates there's a package on its way to you, and the details are in an attached file.

Perhaps your online email provider has detected a problem with your account, and you need to check something by clicking on the conveniently provided link.

I've even received email from "PayPal" indicating that access to my account had been "limited" because of suspicious activity. I needed to log in to provide additional information—once again, using the provided link.[1]

In each case, the sender wants you to trust them, and take whatever action they've recommended in their message, be it examining the contents of an attached file, clicking a provided link to their website, or even replying to the email with sensitive information.

Abusing your trust in this manner is currently one of the most effective ways to distribute malware.

And yet, each one of those scenarios could, in some cases, also be legitimate.

What do you do?

I'm from Microsoft, and we've detected….

You're working on your computer one afternoon and get a phone call from someone who says they work for Microsoft. They've detected that your computer is causing many errors on the internet. They offer to walk you through some steps to show this to you, and indeed, there *do* seem to be lots of unexplained errors right there on your computer.

Then they offer to fix it for you, if you'll just go to a site and type in a few numbers they recite to you.

Those errors are pretty scary looking, and you certainly don't understand them.

What do you do?

What you do: get skeptical

If there were one skill I could magically impart to my *Ask Leo!* readers—hell, on the entire technology-using, internet-loving universe—it would be the skill of healthy skepticism.

I don't mean that you believe nothing and trust no one. I mean that you believe, you question, and before you trust, you learn.

Truly, being skeptical is really the only solution to the scenarios I've outlined above.

---

[1] I've actually received this scenario *legitimately*, which really surprised me. Of course, most are scams of some sort.

In each case, it's *critical* that you not blindly trust the information presented to you. In each case, you must question whether or not the person or company at the other end of the message has your best interests in mind. Is the story they're telling accurate? Verifiably accurate? Do you know beyond doubt that they are who they say they are?

> " *Skeptic: a person who has or shows doubt about something.*
> -Merriam Webster

If the answer to any of those questions is "no", or even "I'm not sure", *stop*. Stop and take additional steps make sense to confirm that what you're being told is legitimate.

It might mean some internet research, calling them back, or asking a trusted friend or resource for their opinion.

But if you aren't sure, question everything.

Be more skeptical: it's one skill that can help prevent disasters before they happen, and keep you and your technology safe.

Nullius in verba: "Take nobody's word for it."[2]

It's more than just technology

Naturally, my plea for being skeptical and that you "question everything" is about far more than just the technology you have sitting in front of you.

As I've written before,[3] an amazing amount of information we're shown each day is completely bogus—or at least nuanced and presented in such a way as to cause you to believe that things are other than they truly are.

Add to that our natural tendency to believe that which supports what we already believe (known as the "echo chamber"), and it's exceptionally easy to be misled and misinformed.

The solution remains the same:

Be skeptical.

Question everything...

...even things you already believe are true.

---

[2] Nullius in verba, besides being the motto of The President, Council, and Fellows of the Royal Society of London for Improving Natural Knowledge, is a very fancy way of saying "question everything". ☺
[3] https://askleo.com/11287

Just What Is Common Sense?

When it comes to internet safety, one of the most oft-cited pieces of advice computer professionals hand out is this:

Use common sense.

One of the most common responses is this:

"Just what does that mean?"

When it comes to technology and safety, "common sense" is incredibly important, poorly defined, and quite *un*common.

Let's see if we can define it with some already-familiar rules.

Common sense can be summed up in several familiar adages:

- If it sounds too good to be true, it's probably not true.
- If it ain't broke, don't fix it.
- Free is never free.
- Read what's in front of you.
- Don't believe everything you read.
- Be skeptical; question everything.
- Do your research.

If it sounds too good to be true...

As we see so often, many malicious incursions mask themselves in promises of things that seem irresistible.

Practical examples of offers that really are too good to be true include:
- Many "free download" advertisements.
- Software that promises to speed up your computer.
- Ads that include the phrase "one stupid trick to..." or variants thereof.
- Click-bait headlines that include the phrase "you won't believe" or "will blow your mind", or similar.

Common to most of these items, beyond the fact that the promises they make seem extreme, is that *you weren't looking for them when you found them.*

Look at any website and you'll see advertisements. Many are legit and well positioned, but many others are little more than over-the-top attempts to get you to click or download whatever they have to offer.

Particularly when you're not looking specifically for something, don't fall for extreme or outlandish claims. They are:
- All too common

- Very often completely false

The same can be said of most forwarded hoaxes and urban legends, as well as many "news" stories on not-quite-reputable (or even satire) sites.

Common sense tells us if it promises too much, if it seems too extreme, if it seems too astonishing … then it's probably completely false. Don't waste your time.

If it ain't broke, don't fix it

Often following over-inflated promises such as those I just mentioned, or out of desperation, I often see people trying to do things to their computers that, quite simply, have nothing to do with a problem they're experiencing.

- They're trying to solve speed problems they don't have.
- They're trying to remove malware that isn't present.
- They're trying to update software they don't use.
- They're trying to fix problems that have nothing to do with their computer.

The list goes on.

Now, I get that each of those assumes a certain amount of knowledge. How do you know you don't have a specific problem? How do you know that malware isn't present? How do you know the problem you're experiencing is with the website you visit, and has nothing to do with your computer?

That's a fair concern. But if you don't know you have a problem, why are you trying to fix it?

So turn the thinking around.

Common sense means not doing something because you might have a problem, but taking action because you know you have a problem, and not before.

Research the problem first. Confirm you actually have a problem that needs fixing before you try to fix it.

I'll talk about research shortly.

Free is never free

The old economist's acronym is TANSTAAFL: "There ain't no such thing as a free lunch." That's exceptionally true on the internet.

Every "free" service has a cost. It may be the advertising you need to look at, it may be the mailing list you need to sign up for, or it may be something else entirely, but there is no such thing as "free" on the internet.

Most commonly, people fall into the "free" trap through advertisements of this variety: "FREE scan! Scan your computer for malware for FREE!"

In reality, the advertisement is 100% completely accurate. The *scan* is completely free. The not-so-free part? If you want to do anything about what the scan finds, you'll need to pay. It's a common sales tactic.

Less reputable programs actually lie to you. They warn you of malware and other scary things that you don't have or aren't issues—all making it appear that giving them your money is the only way to avoid certain doom.

Which brings us to another important point.

Read what's in front of you

This is a point that frustrates me. It works like this:
- A program fails or something goes wrong.
- The user reacts, gets frustrated, or gets lost.
- The user completely misses the fact that *the solution to the issue was included* in the error message or descriptive text.

Another similar scenario:
- Someone gets an email and reads the first line, which is so outrageous that their reactions kick in right there and they stop reading.
- As a result, they miss the text that follows, which removes all outrageousness by putting the statement in a clearer context or providing additional information.

When it comes to your computer, when something goes wrong, please *take the time to read what's on the screen in front of you*. That really is only good, common sense. I get so many questions that could be quickly dealt with had the questioner just slowed down and read the instructions in front of them.

I get that those instructions are not always comprehensible. Honestly, I do. But sometimes they really are so clear and obvious that just taking the time to slow down and carefully read what's on your screen will get you a long, long way.

Which brings us to the flip side of the coin.

Don't believe everything you read

I'm a firm believer that people are basically good.[4]

But that doesn't mean that everyone is good, or that everyone has your best interests in mind ...

... particularly when it comes to the internet.

---

[4] That's one reason I took on heroicstories.org and run notallnewsisbad.com.

It's simply too easy, particularly in today's exceptionally connected and information-rich world, to spread misinformation as fact. We see it all the time.

Misleading ads are only one blatant example. The reality is that misleading ads pre-date the internet by decades, if not hundreds, of years. It's just that today's technology often makes it difficult to distinguish snake oil from valuable and effective medication unless we're careful.

In reality, the internet can provide us with a wealth of information to help us separate over-inflated claims from reality.

It can also provide us with even more misinformation.

"It's on the internet so it must be true" is one of those statements that everyone laughs at because it's so blatantly wrong, it's laughable. Common sense tells us that just because something is on the internet has absolutely no bearing on its accuracy. Yet we see people act as if it's completely accurate, believing random and misleading statements from vague sources with a less-than-altruistic agenda.

With information coming at you from so many random directions, from sources both reliable and unreliable, it's critical we do not believe everything we read just because it's been formatted prettily[5] on a site that looks authoritative.

And that brings us to the most important point of all.

Above all, be skeptical

Want something that's very common sense? Question everything …

… even me.

Never accept information at face value, particularly on the internet, and particularly from sites or individuals you've never heard of before.

Be skeptical. Ask questions. Consider the source, and what that source's agenda[6] might be in spreading its message. Are they being truthful?

Over time, develop a set of resources that you trust. Naturally, I hope *Ask Leo!* will be one of them, but honestly, what matters more is that you reach out and find sites, sources, services, and individuals that you trust.

Then use those resources to help you evaluate the constant stream of information and misinformation that's heading your way.

Yes, it's a little bit of work. But it's critical.

---

[5] Also not new. I'm fairly certain that my good grade on a paper I turned in while in college was due to the fact I'd figured out how to use a word processor to make it look much better than it actually was.
[6] And don't kid yourself, every source has an agenda. More here: Stop spreading manure.

Do your research!

Search for yourself. Learn the basics[7] of how to not only use a good search engine (Google, Bing, or others), but also how best to interpret the results. Understand the difference between advertisements presented on the search results page and the actual results (see image at right).

Look for well-known, reputable sites you recognize in those results, not just sites that happen to rank highly. As much as the search engines work to make it not so, ranking highly in a search result is not an indication that the site is legitimate or trustworthy.

If you choose to look at information presented by a site you've never heard of before, remember, you've never heard of it before! Without more research, there's no way to know whether or not the information presented is valid, biased, or completely bogus.

Get help. If you're uncertain how to go about researching a particular topic, there's nothing wrong in asking for help. You may have more experienced friends or family members who can help you find what you're looking for. Many librarians have become valuable resources when trying to understand how best to determine the validity of information you run across online.

Regardless of who's helping you, it's still okay to be skeptical. When they suggest a site as a trustworthy resource, don't be afraid to ask them why they trust it.

Look carefully for confirmation. There are two types of "confirmation":
- Source "B" repeating what source "A" has said
- Source "B" independently presenting the similar information or conclusion that source "A" did

The first isn't confirmation at all; it's repetition. The problem is, when enough sites and so-called sources all repeat what only one of them has said, it may feel like many sources have come to the same conclusion. In reality, it's nothing more than a single opinion repeated over and over. This is known as the "echo chamber".

Remember that *repetition isn't confirmation*. You want to find multiple sources that confirm or deny the issue, and do so having arrived at their conclusions *independently*, using their own research and work.

---

[7] https://askleo.com/two-steps-better-search-results/

Use debunking sites. I'm a huge believer in using sites like snopes.com,[8] urbanlegends.about.com, factcheck.org, or any of several others before reacting to the latest over-the-top, can't-possibly-be-true news story, tech tip, or emailed rumor. Many are very timely and do the kind of research you want to see before getting all excited or worked up about what just landed in your inbox.

Use resource sites. For just about any topic, there are resource sites. Develop a set of sites that you trust. For example, when it comes to technology, I would hope you trust *Ask Leo!* Visit the sites you already trust to see what they say about the issue at hand. As always, I'm not saying you need to trust them completely, but use them as part of your research to develop your own well-thought-out opinions.

The bottom line is this: if something you run across is worth the effort to take any action at all—even if it's just to forward an email—it's also worth researching first. At worst, it may save you some embarrassment. At best, it could protect your computer, your identity, and even your possessions.

---

[8] No, Snopes isn't left-wing biased. Generally people claiming so are simply unhappy with the truth Snopes has uncovered. Nonetheless, if you're not happy with Snopes, look at any of the multiple debunking sites that are available these days.

Stop Spreading Manure

In an example of yet another brouhaha, supposedly in a report a few years ago, Google blatantly admitted that you should have no expectation of privacy whatsoever when using their services. The internet went crazy. Many sources seemed to say, "How outrageous! We told you so! Google is evil!" Mainstream news outlets picked up stories from smaller publishers, and they all seemed to confirm the entire sordid mess.

Except the internet was wrong. Manure, to use a polite term, was being spread far, wide, and fast.

This is where things get complicated.

Everyone Has an Agenda

In the popular television series *House,*[9] Dr. Gregory House often says, "Everyone lies."

On the internet, a similar statement can be made: everyone has an agenda.

Every website, news organization, and person sending an email, publishing a newsletter, or posting a comment has an agenda of some sort. They have something they want you to do, think, or become.[10]

All too often, the agenda being promoted is ... *inconsistent* (for lack of a better word) with reality.

In other words, the information you present is almost always colored by your agenda. People highlight facts supporting a particular agenda, conveniently minimizing or ignoring facts that don't. In the worst case, people fabricate "facts" to support their agenda.

Yes: not everyone, but some people, lie. Perhaps more often than you think.

To be honest, we all do it: we color what we say and do with data to support what we believe, often to the exclusion of all evidence pointing out the unthinkable:... we might be wrong.

If It's on the Internet, It Must Be ...

There's an interesting and somewhat strange conflict in our culture these days.

---

[9] http://www.imdb.com/title/tt0412142/

[10] My agenda is simple: I want you to be more skeptical before you believe what you see on the internet, and I want you to stop spreading misinformation. I'd love for this article to go viral and garner more Ask Leo! newsletter subscribers and site visitors, as well as improving my site's reputation with Google. I have a large agenda. And don't think for a moment that other sites, services, and individuals don't have agendas that are as large or larger.

Most people realize that "If it's on the internet, it must be true" is a sarcastic falsism expressing just how inaccurate information on the internet can be. Just because it's published on a website somewhere (or shows up in your inbox, on Facebook, or wherever), doesn't make it true.

However, I would wager that most people *do* believe most of what they read on the internet. Those same people smiling knowingly at that falsism go on to believe the strangest, most bizarre, completely false things, as long as the information is presented in a seemingly credible way.

They do it without thinking and without seeing the irony in their behavior.

From what I've seen, this is getting worse.

We Believe What We Want to Believe

There are a couple of terms that help explain, at least in part, why that might be.

Confirmation bias is the natural tendency we all have to believe what confirms what we already believe and dismiss what doesn't. Confirmation bias can be as simple as dismissing alternative viewpoints out of hand, and as horrific as being tried and arrested for expressing beliefs that are not commonly accepted (think Galileo[11]).

The problem with confirmation bias, as Galileo so clearly illustrates, is that it often stands in the way of the truth.

Put another way, we believe what we want to believe. We believe what matches our own world view and our own agenda, *whether or not we are right.*

The *echo chamber* is a term we've been hearing more and more in recent years. It's the tendency of information sources—most notably news media—to repeat each other. In a sense, they use each other as sources. The problem is that a story originating from a single source—be it true or false—can appear to have massive objective confirmation when we start hearing that same story from a variety of supposedly independent sources.

Those sources aren't independent at all; they're just repeating what they heard from each other.

And it all started from a single source ...

... a source with an agenda.

Fifty Shades of Gray

Things get more complicated still.

---

[11] https://go.askleo.com/galileo

We desperately want things to be simple. We want things to be true or false, black or white, right or wrong ...

... good or evil.

It's much easier to comprehend "true" and "false" than it is to deal with the potential uncertainty of "mostly true", "kind of wrong", or something in between. Unlike whether the sun circles the earth or the other way around, the issues that we consider, discuss, and even rant about are rarely so simple as to have easy yes/no, black or white answers.

The folks who write headlines and push agendas know that thinking is hard for many of us. They know that black and white is easier, and (bonus!) much more sensational. So, they simply pick and choose the "facts" that support black-and-white thinking at the exclusion of the significantly more nuanced truth.

About that Google Privacy Thing

So is your email private with Google or not?

It's not that simple. It's still not a yes-or-no answer.

And yet:
- Organizations believed to have an anti-Google bias[12]
  - Drew a sensational black or white conclusion[13]
    - Based on a quote taken without complete and proper context
      - Which was then bounced around the echo chamber on sites here[14], here[15] , here[16] and dozens of other media sites. [17]

Even though some sites posted clarifications and/or updates, they're often did so too late (the misinformation had spread) or too little (the "clarifications" remain biased to the pre-existing story or overall agenda).

Email privacy, and privacy on the internet in general, is a critically important concept. Services like Gmail do process your email to do things like serve related ads that pay for the free service, or populate indexes so you can search your email quickly. Are there teams of people sitting behind computer monitors reading your email? Almost certainly not.

---

[12] http://www.pcworld.com/article/204842/consumer_watchdog_fighting_google.html

[13] http://www.consumerwatchdog.org/newsrelease/google-tells-court-you-cannot-expect-privacy-when-sending-messages-gmail-people-who-care

[14] http://techland.time.com/2013/08/14/google-says-gmail-users-have-no-legitimate-expectation-of-privacy/

[15] http://www.huffingtonpost.com/2013/08/13/gmail-privacy_n_3751971.html

[16] http://www.sfgate.com/technology/businessinsider/article/GOOGLE-If-You-Use-Gmail-You-Have-No-Legitimate-4730587.php

[17] These three were selected at random from an (irony alert) Google News search on "Google Privacy".

However, unless you encrypt your email, it is by definition fundamentally not secure. *This is nothing new,* or specific to Google.

And yet, in the pursuit of clicks, page views, and furthering anti-Google sentiment, some sources pick and choose what to present, and then sensationalize how they present it.

You. Must. Think.

So what's the solution?

You. You are the solution. You and I and everyone we know must—and I really do mean *must*—become more skeptical and demanding of our news and information sources.

You and I must THINK about what we read. We need to learn to identify the sources and the agendas those sources have that color what they present and how they present it.

We need to learn to draw our own conclusions.

Whenever you accept misleading or inaccurate stories as truth, *you've been manipulated* to serve someone else's agenda. And when you pass those manipulative stories on to friends, family, and acquaintances? Well, my friend, you've just turned into a virtual manure spreader.

Because manure is what it is.

Be skeptical.[18]

If it sounds outrageous—*even if it supports your beliefs*—there's a hefty chance *it's completely bogus.* Overly sensational or outrageous-sounding headlines or content are a hallmark of bogus stories.

Do a little research. Check and verify the sources—follow the trail. If they all point back to a single source (or no source at all), realize what you're looking at. One source repeated a thousand times in a thousand places doesn't make it a thousand sources.

In the past, we could count on the media to do fact- and source-checking for us, but that's clearly no longer true. In the race for media outlets to publish quickly, the effort to make sure it's accurate has apparently been left behind.

Collateral Damage: Legitimate News and Important Issues

One of the truly sad casualties of all the misinformation on the internet is how difficult it has become to find the truth ...

... and how difficult it is for accurate, important news and information to get the attention it truly deserves.

It's all lost in the noise: covered in manure.

---

[18] https://askleo.com/21535

The non-profit world has a term: "donor fatigue". This applies to potential contributors who, while supportive of a cause or organization, get tired of being asked for money, time, or whatever repeatedly.

The same is true here.

Call it "manure fatigue". It would be tempting to completely disregard anything found on the internet as likely being bogus.

Unfortunately, there are legitimate outrages, atrocities, and issues of privacy[19] that really do deserve our attention, understanding, and even action.

It just takes some skepticism and some thought to separate the wheat from the fertilizer.

---

[19] https://askleo.com/21593

Part 2. Protect Your Data

How Do I Back Up My Computer?

> " *How do I "back up" my computer? I am sure my question is ridiculous to you, but I honestly have no clue what I should be doing.*

Your question isn't ridiculous at all. In fact, I'm certain it's one reason so many people don't back up: they simply don't know how.

For something as critically important as backing up, that's more than a little scary. I hear from people who've lost important and valuable information all the time. Whether it's from malware, hardware failure, account hacks, or other disasters, a backup could easily prevent such loss.

First, let's look at what it means to back up a computer, and what your options are. Then, I'll share some guidelines and tell you what I recommend for typical users.

Backing up

To back something up is to make a *copy* of it, and then keep that copy in a safe place.

That's it. Nothing more, nothing less.

The key word in that statement is "copy", as in duplicating the information. After you back up, you have the same information in two or more places.

That leads to my most important rule:

If it's in only one place, it's not backed up.

Folks occasionally misunderstand the concept. After copying their information to their "backup" drive, they delete the original. That means there's still only one copy: the one on that backup drive. Regardless of what you call the drive it's on, *if it's in only one place,* it's not backed up.

The purpose of a backup is simple: if something happens and you can't get your information from your computer or online account (which happens much more often than you probably realize), then you get the information from the backed-up copies—you haven't lost it forever.

Backing up starts to seem complicated when you look at all the options related to how much to back up, how often, and what tools to use to make sure it happens regularly.

Types of backups

Backing up generally takes one of two forms.

- Copying your data. If you copy pictures from your digital camera to your computer without deleting them from the camera, that's a backup. If you then burn those pictures to a DVD for safekeeping, you've backed them up again. Similarly, if you take the contents of your "My Documents" folder tree and copy it to another machine or burn it to DVD, you've backed those files up.
- Imaging your system. Rather than backing up this and that, hoping you're including everything that might be important, a full-image backup copies *absolutely everything* your data, your programs, your settings, and even the computer's operating system itself.

Both types of backups share two important characteristics:

1. The backup creates a *copy* of the data.
2. That copy is placed *somewhere else*.

If your data is in only one place, meaning that there are *no copies* of that data, then you're not backed up.

Backup locations

So where should this "somewhere else" be?

Well, the ideal answer is "as far away from your computer as practical."

The further your backup lives from the original, the more types of disasters you'll be protected from.

- If the backup is on the same hard disk, and that hard disk dies, you could lose your data *and your backup*.
- If the backup is on a different hard disk inside the same computer, and something happens to the computer that causes both hard disks to be harmed (like a power supply failure), you could lose your data *and your backup*.
- If the backup is on an external hard disk but connected to the same computer, and there's a software glitch or malware on that computer that starts destroying files on all connected devices, you could lose your data *and your backup*.
- If the backup is on a different computer on the same network, a network problem or malware on your local network could start deleting files, including your data *and your backup*.
- If the backup is copied to a DVD, USB stick, or external drive and kept in the same *physical* location, and that location suffers a physical catastrophe such as a fire or flood, you could lose your data *and your backup*.

The closer your backup is to the original, the greater the possibility you could lose both at once.

It doesn't happen often, but it can.

Backing up in 3, 2, 1...

A great overall strategy for backing up is what many refer to as the "3, 2, 1" approach.
- 3 copies
- 2 different formats
- 1 copy kept off-site

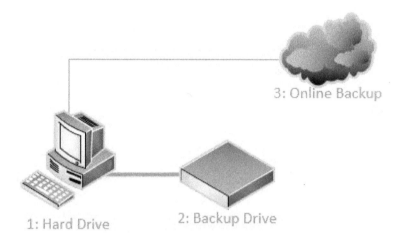

Three copies

If a backup is "a" copy, why are we suddenly talking about *three* copies?

Because stuff happens. Backups fail, and if you believe in fate (or Finagle's law[20]), they'll fail just when you need them most.

If for no other reason, consider this scenario:
- You have a (single) copy of your data as a backup. Good for you. :-)
- Your hard disk dies and all data on it is lost. But you have your backup!
- But ... now you have *only* your backup—a single copy of your data.

Without your original hard disk, your data is in only one place. Until you make another copy, *it's not backed up...*

... unless you had your data in three places. Then you could lose any single copy and still be backed up.

Two formats

Every possible backup approach carries some risk of failure. Nothing is ever perfect.

---

[20] https://go.askleo.com/finagle

For example, CDs and DVDs, USB sticks, external drives, and on-line backups are all subject to different types of risks of failure.

Using more than one type of backup is all about reducing the risk of a backup not being there when you need it.

One off-site

As we saw earlier, the further your backup copy is from the original, the more you're protected. In particular, many people overlook the risk of theft or physical disasters (such as fire) to the data they have in their home or business.

Storing critical data somewhere else—somewhere else *physically* —means that no matter what happens to your computer or the backups you're creating onsite, you'll always be able to recover the information kept elsewhere.

But how do I do all that?

Even with these guidelines, the original question remains: just *how* should you back up?

The questions that drive your answer are:
- How likely is it that something will happen to your data?
- How important is your data?

From my experience, I will say that the answers tend to be:
- More likely than you think.
- More important than you think.

The three most data-loss scenarios I see people go through are:
- Malware
- Hard drive failure
- Accidental deletion

Without fail, they're surprised that it happened to them. What happens next depends on how well they prepared.

Protecting yourself against at least those three scenarios is a great place to start.

A 1, 2, 3 suggested backup plan

There are many approaches to backing up. Rather than trying to cover them all, I'll make a simple suggestion that will work well for most.

1. Get an external USB hard disk

The first question that probably comes to mind is "how big?". There's no blanket answer, but I'll throw out this guideline:

Examine your computer's hard drive using Windows Explorer and determine how much data is on the drive.

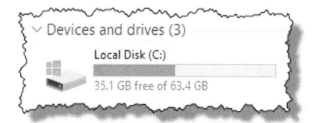

If your 64 gigabyte hard drive has 35 gigabytes free, that means that you have 29 gigabytes of data stored on that drive.

Get a hard disk at least four times bigger. Using my example, I'd get (29 times 4) at least 116GB.

As I write this, it would actually be difficult to get a drive that *small*, given that drives are now more commonly measured in terabytes, or 1000 gigabytes. Your numbers will vary, of course, but when in doubt, go big; there's no such thing as a drive that's "too big".

2. Get backup software

I strongly recommend using a dedicated, automated backup program like Macrium Reflect,[21] EaseUS Todo,[22] or an equivalent to create image backups on your external drive automatically on a daily or weekly schedule. (You can use the backup software included in Windows, but to be honest, I find these dedicated tools to be more reliable, more flexible, and, most importantly, more transparent in their operations.)

3. Backup data online

Use a service like Microsoft OneDrive, Dropbox, or others to automatically backup your most important data, including the files and folders you're working on day-to-day.

These tools are primarily data-sharing tools; their primary purpose is to replicate your data across multiple machines, as well as on their own web-based interfaces. Because they make your files available online, these services copy your data to their servers.

In other words, it's an easy and often nearly-instant "somewhere else" to back up your data.

Now, to be clear, this recommendation won't protect you from absolutely *everything*, but it will protect you from a lot. In fact, it'll save you from what I see almost every day as the most common causes of data loss.

If your hard disk dies, you can restore files (and perhaps the entire system) from your backup. If you happen to—oops!—delete a file by accident, as long as it was there when the most recent

---

[21] https://askleo.com/4996
[22] https://go.askleo.com/todofree

backup was taken, you can restore it quickly and easily. If malware strikes, you can restore your system from a backup taken prior to the infection.

Most programs come with relatively simple instructions to set up the most common types of backups for average users.

Starting with the 1, 2, 3 approach provides you a good base. If the importance of your data requires stronger measures, you can build from there.

What Backup Program Should I Use?

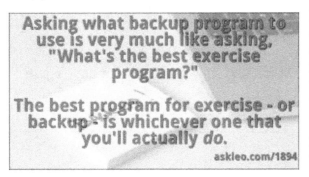
Asking what backup program to use is very much like asking, "What's the best exercise program?"

The best program for exercise - or backup - is whichever one that you'll actually *do*.

askleo.com/1894

Backing up is kind of like eating healthier: everyone knows we should, and few of us actually do. Much like the heart attack victim who no longer binges on French fries, when it comes to backing up, the most religious are those who've been bitten hard by a failure in their past.

Asking what backup program to use is very much like asking, "What's the best exercise program?"

The best program for exercise—or backup—is whichever one you'll actually do. In order to choose what's going to work best for you, there are several questions to ask.

Do I want to put a lot of thought into this?

If this isn't something you want to spend some time learning about—and to be honest, most people don't—then prepare to spend a little more money for some additional disk space and get a good, dedicated backup program.

Hardware is continually changing, but I'm still pleased with my external USB Maxtor drive.

In addition to a drive, you'll need a backup program. Many external drives come with backup software of some sort; that's sometimes a good place to start. Unfortunately, while the drive may be good, you don't always know the quality of the free software included with it.

If, as I recommend, you elect to get backup software, there are many good choices. I personally use and recommend Macrium Reflect or EaseUS Todo for most home users. (There are both paid and free versions of each.) Starting with Windows 7 (though apparently being de-emphasized in later versions of Windows 10), the backup program included with Windows appears also worthy of consideration.

Am I comfortable re-installing my system?

This is a comfort-versus-space tradeoff.

If you're okay with re-installing your system from scratch, which means your operating system as well as all applications and customizations, and you can clearly identify what does and doesn't need to be saved, you can save a lot of disk space by backing up only your data. This requires a great deal of diligence on your part, because anything you don't specify to be backed up will be lost in the case of a catastrophic failure.

Either way, you need to make sure to use a technique—either home-brewed or in the form of a backup or automated copy program—to make sure this happens automatically. Relying on your memory to back up isn't typically the best choice.

Is there another machine nearby?

You might not have to go out of your way to get additional hardware for back-up purposes.

Hard disks are so large these days that simply having another machine on your local network with sufficient free space can be a quick and easy solution. Many back-up programs allow you to back up across a network. Having two machines back each other up is a quick way to ensure that if either has a problem, your data is safe on the other.

This does mean you'll have to set up your local network and enable file sharing on it—something that isn't always the easiest to accomplish or maintain.[23]

How valuable is what you're doing?

What if your building, including your machines and all of their backups, was lost in a fire?

If the potential data loss just sent a shiver down your spine, you might consider *off-site* data storage for your backups. That could mean periodically taking an external disk with your backups on it to some other location, or if the sizes are small enough, backing up across the network to a server not in your home.

When my wife had a retail store, I had an external drive for backups at her store, another in our home and would periodically simply swap the two. Each location then had "offsite" backup at the other.

In recent years, another approach might be even easier....

Might an online backup program be an option?

If the amount of data you're backing up is manageable, and your internet connection is relatively fast, an online backup system may be worth considering.

These programs back up your critical files to secure servers on the internet, giving you both data and off-site backup at the same time. In addition, some services allow you to access your backed-up files from any machine connected to the internet. This approach is impractical for large backups (such as full image or complete system backups) due to upload speed and storage size limitations.

You might also consider services like Dropbox, OneDrive, Google Drive, and others. Data placed in folders managed by these services is automatically backed up[24] to their servers (and to any other computers you install the software on, should you choose).

How important is incremental access?

How important is it that you be able to recover a file from a specific day, and not a day before or after? If you simply back up all your files on top of previous versions, you'll only have the most

---

[23] https://askleo.com/2441
[24] https://askleo.com/29368

recent version. In many, many cases, that's enough. In some cases, it's not; one example might be needing to recover an older version of a file that became corrupt at some point.

What resources should I back up?

Have you thought about *all* your computers? All the drives therein? How about external hard drives you're not using for backup? Do you have a website? Do you have a backup of it? What would happen if your ISP "lost" it? (It's happened.) If you're a small business, do you have databases that need backing up? Office machines that belong to everyone but no one?

My answers, and one possible approach

These questions can seem overwhelming. Actually deciding what to do can be agonizing.

But I really, really want you to take action and ensure that your precious data is backed up somehow, somewhere. I hear too often from too many people who have lost too much. It's downright heartbreaking at times.

So here's one possible approach that should work well for a large number of home and small business users.
1. Equip each computer with an external drive, at least four times as large as the amount of spaced currently used on the computer's existing drive(s).
2. Install an image backup program such as Macrium Reflect[25] or EaseUS Todo.[26]
3. Configure that program to take monthly full-image backups and daily incremental images.[27]
4. Discard backups older than two months. (This can often be done automatically.)
5. Install a data-sharing program, such as DropBox[28] or OneDrive[29] or similar, and store your data files in folders managed by the program for automatic off-site and cloud backup of the files you work on every day.

I'll call this an 80% solution: something that will work, and work well for most people. Naturally, it won't be exactly right for some, but it's a start.

The bottom line for backing up is simple: *just do it*. Understand what you have and what you're willing to invest in, but do *something*... before it's too late.

---

[25] https://askleo.com/4996
[26] https://askleo.com/29600
[27] I have various articles with basic details on each, simply search Ask Leo! for the tool you want to try. The best resources are my books on each: Saved! Backing Up with EaseUS Todo and Saved! Backing Up with Macrium Reflect.
[28] https://askleo.com/4540
[29] https://askleo.com/18583

Can't I Just Copy Everything to Back Up?

> **"**
> *For security in case of a crash, can I just copy my whole hard drive to an external drive as a backup rather than using a backup program? At the present time I am just copying My Documents to a flash drive, but am concerned that to recover I would have to rebuild all the files and updates if I had a crash.*

Sure. You can do that: just copy everything. It provides a level of protection, and it's significantly better than doing nothing at all.

But your safety net has some extremely large holes in it.

There are things a "copy everything" backup misses that a traditional backup program would catch—things you'll really care about when the worst happens.

Copy everything to another drive

To be clear, the scenario here is that you're attempting to backup C: by just copying *all* of it to The scenario proposed here is backing up C: by just copying all of it to an external drive, like F:. If you're familiar with Windows Command Prompt, it might look something like this:

C:> xcopy /e /h c:\ f:\

There may be other options that would make sense, but I've included the important ones to copy the contents of all files and folders from the root of the C: drive to the root of the F: drive, and copy hidden and system files as well. It would have to be run "as administrator" to pick up files that normal accounts don't have access to.

In theory, it seems simple, and in many ways it's conceptually close to what a backup program does.

But there are some important things missing.

What copying "everything" misses

There are files that will not be backed up by this approach.

Most importantly, many[30] files open in running programs at the time of the backup will not be copied.

And some files are always in use.

The most notable may be the Windows registry—the storehouse of settings and configurations used by Windows and installed applications. If Windows is running, the files containing the registry are locked from outside access.

---

[30] Some will be, but many will not. It depends on the restrictions placed on the files when they are opened by the programs involved.

Without the registry, if your hard drive were to die, you're still looking at a complete reinstall of Windows, followed by a complete reinstall of your applications, onto a replacement drive.

The registry is just the tip of the iceberg. When running, Windows has many other files open, preventing you from backing up them with a simple copy/paste. Other applications may also be running with locked and uncopyable open files.

A back-up program really can copy everything

Backup programs[31] use functionality specifically designed to give them access to protected files and files in use.

In other words, a backup program copies *everything*.

There are a couple of other less-critical-yet-handy benefits to using a backup program.

Most backup programs easy to "set and forget". Once configured, they run and back up automatically. Yes, you should test your backups,[32] but you won't have to waste much energy thinking about them on a regular basis; they just happen.

But there's an interesting scenario in which a backup program can save the day that doesn't involve a hard-disk crash or other catastrophic failures.

How "copy everything" backups lose files

Imagine this scenario:

You create an important file. I'll call this version 1.
- Your nightly file copy backup backs it up.
- The next day, you make changes to the file, creating version 2.
- Your nightly file copy backup backs it up, overwriting version 1 in the backup.
- The next day you realize that those changes to version 2 were a horrible, horrible mistake.
- You really want version 1 back. Except it's gone. It's been overwritten everywhere, including your backup, by version 2.

Had you been using a good backup program, that scenario may have had a different outcome.

Incremental backups

Imagine this scenario instead:

---

[31] https://askleo.com/1894
[32] https://askleo.com/20591

- You create an important file. Once again, it's version 1.
- Your backup software creates a full image backup of your hard drive, including the file.
- The next day, you make changes to the file to create version 2.
- Your backup software creates an *incremental* backup, backing up only those files that have changed since the previous backup, including version 2.
- The next day, that same realization hits: version 2 was a disaster, and you need to revert to version 1.

In this scenario, you can. An incremental backup has two important differences over the "copy everything" approach:

1. It only adds files to the backup, never deletes them.
2. It only adds those files that have changed since the previous backup.

That means that version 1 of your file is still there, ready to be recovered with your backup software.

Incremental in practice

I configure my backup software to:

- Create a full image backup of everything once a month.
- Create an incremental image backup each night of everything that changed that day.
- Save backups for at least two months.

That means I can revert any file to the state it was in any day in the preceding 60 days.

Now, aside from the "files in use" problem I talked about earlier, you could probably devise a system using batch files and copy operations to mimic much of this. But a backup program is more reliable, easier to use, and in my opinion, worth every penny.[33]

"Copy everything" can work sometimes

To be fair, there are scenarios where simple file copies work, and work well enough.

For example, I have some drives that contain *only* data, and no files are in use in the middle of the night. I just copy or "mirror" those drives to other drives nightly using a simple file copy operation, much like the command line example shown above. There's no need for a more sophisticated backup, and the mirrored drive is simply there, on my network, ready to be used at any time.

Copying files to backup can also be a space saver under two conditions:

- You know—and I mean *really* know—which files should be backed up and which you don't need. Often that's as simple as having all of your data on a separate drive, partition, or folder.

    and

---

[33] Which can often be no pennies at all, since there are free solutions.

- Your system drive is either backed up using a backup program, or you plan on reinstalling the operating system and all applications from scratch in the case of a catastrophic failure.

It's a completely valid way to back up, as long as you *know* it's sufficient for your situation. It's important to realize that for many people, a complete reinstall would mean a couple of days of lost work, whereas a backup program could have taken care of it in an hour or so.

And that brings me to my final point about using copy operations as backups: restoration.

Restoring your copied files

As we've seen from our original example, a "reverse copy" of the backup on F: back to C: would not restore your system. Certain critical files, such as the registry, would be missing. Your "restored" drive would not be able to boot. You could recover data files from your backup, and perhaps some other files, but that's about it. It wouldn't restore your entire *system*.

If your intent is to back up everything, so in the case of a failure you can simply and quickly replace a hard drive and restore *everything*, then a good backup program is the only way to go.

For a complete overview of one approach to backing up properly, have a look at How to Back Up Windows 10.[34]

---

[34] https://askleo.com/30103

How Do I Test Backups? Three Practical Steps to Make Sure the Safety Net Will Work

> **"**
> *I do backups of my data using Windows but it's not maybe as retrievable as I would like it to be. I don't know exactly how to test backups to know whether they're really there. It says they are but are they? I've had to use the system image to restore function once when my computer became infected with something. I basically just transferred the system image back to my C drive and it solved all my problems. I must say I'm thankful to you for strongly encouraging everyone to do backups. I can't tell you how many friends and family have lost stuff – everything – because of not backing up. Pictures, important data. Loss of pictures seems to be the most heartbreaking..*

Yeah, I hear those heartbreaking stories all the time, and yes, it is indeed one of the reasons that I talk so much about backing up.

Your concern about backups are common, as is the desire to test.

Let's review how you can get a little bit of confidence that what you have will be there when you need it.

A full restore is the ultimate test

The ultimate way to test backups, of course, is exactly what you ended up doing: performing a full restore of an image backup.

A full restore is the most important to have work, since it's what can save you from almost any problem. Malware infection? Restore to an image created before the infection, and it's gone. Hardware failure? Replace the drive, restore the most recent image, and you're up and working again.

The problem in testing backups is that a full restore is really, really risky.

By definition, a full restore is a destructive operation. By that, I mean it erases what's currently on the hard drive and replaces it with the contents of the backup image. If that operation fails part way through, you're actually worse off than when you began. You found out that your backup didn't work, but you trashed what was on the hard drive in the process.

The very restore you would want to be able to fix that failure is the restore your test just discovered doesn't work!

So, here's my approach to test backups.

Use the rescue media, prepare for a restore, and stop

Create the rescue media — sometimes called an "emergency disc" — from your backup program. This is the CD, DVD, or USB stick you would boot from in order to perform that full restore. Then boot from it.

Getting this to work is important, because booting from something other than your hard drive can be complicated, particularly in newer machines.[35]

Once the software on the rescue media is running, make sure it can see the drive that contains your backup images.

Then follow the steps to do an image restore, **stopping** at the very last step before the restore would begin. This verifies that your recovery disk works, and that the backup program can access what's necessary to perform the restore.

That's about as far as you can go without actually performing the restore, but you've tested quite a bit.

Extract files

Most backup programs allow you to extract individual files from your full system backup image. Doing so is another way to test backups.

I recommend simply restoring a single file.

Exactly how to do that varies depending on what backup program you're running, but the scenario is the same: delete or rename an unimportant file on your hard disk, and go through the steps for your backup program to restore it from a backup.

You shouldn't need to boot from the rescue media—this is something you can typically do by running the backup software and using it to extract individual files from wherever your backups are stored.

If you succeed, great! You now have a relatively good level of confidence that the files contained in that backup image can be restored in the event of an actual disaster.

If you fail, however, you know you need to revisit how you're backing up to make sure you're backing up what you need in the appropriate way.

---

[35] https://askleo.com/5356

Check the image

There's one final test I like to perform to make sure the files you think are in your backup are in fact in your backup.

For example, in my Maximum Reflect book,[36] I outline how to mount a backup image as a virtual hard drive. You can do this with Windows 7 backup as well. Then you can examine the entire contents of the image to make sure it contains what you expect.

Poke around in the backed-up Windows folders to make sure all of Windows is there. Browse through the folders that contain your data to ensure the same. Look around inside that image to ensure it has what you might need should the worst ever happen.

There is no 100% guarantee that your backup will work when you need it, but these tests can give you confidence that issues that often get in the way of a working backup won't get in the way for you.

A complete test, done safely

There's one more way to test backups that involves more work and some additional cost, but it'll prove, beyond a doubt, that your backups work.
1. Buy a new hard drive.
2. Actually replace the hard drive in your machine with this new hard drive.
3. Restore an image to the new hard drive.
4. Reboot.

If this works, you can leave the new hard drive in your machine and keep the old as a spare.

If it fails, you can simply put the old hard drive back in your machine, and move on to diagnose what failed and why.

---

[36] https://store.askleo.com/saved-macrium-reflect/

Cloud Storage as Cloud Backup: Four Safety Rules

> " *I now have 1 TB of Microsoft OneDrive storage. How should that affect my backup strategy? Most of my data files are now on OneDrive; do those need to be backed up? Can I use OneDrive space as my "external hard drive" for backups of my other files? How about for image backups? Can/should Macrium Reflect put a system image onto OneDrive? Other advice re wise and safe use of cloud storage?*

The availability of lots of cloud storage services has greatly expanded our options for keeping our data both safe and accessible.

While it's expanded our ability to establish cloud backup options, it's also greatly expanded our ability to get it wrong. It's now very easy to think you are backed up when you are not, or to inadvertently expose yourself to additional risks.

Let's review some rules about backing up, and about cloud backup specifically.

Cloud storage vs. cloud backup

We seem to use these terms interchangeably when in reality they're two distinct things. The distinction matters.

Cloud storage is nothing more than an online service into which you can store and later retrieve files. Examples include OneDrive, Dropbox, and others, but can also include your favorite photo-sharing site, your own website, or just about any other online service that can hold files.

Cloud backup specifically uses cloud storage as a place to keep backup copies of your data. You may work on your files on your computer, but some process makes copies of those files and stores them securely online.

Cloud backup solutions typically fall into one of two buckets:

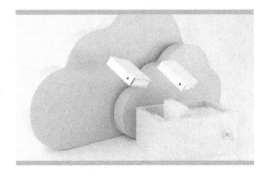

- Tools like Dropbox and OneDrive, which are primarily multi-computer file replication and sharing utilities backing up files almost as a side effect of their utility.
- Dedicated backup services mimicking traditional backup programs by backing up on a schedule using online storage rather than an external drive.

Back up your cloud data

This is *by far* the single most important rule I can offer you. If you remember nothing else, remember this:

If there is only one copy, it's not backed up.

I don't care where you keep your data—on your computer, in the cloud, or somewhere else—if you have only one copy, then by definition, your data is not backed up.

So when you say, "Most of my data files are now on OneDrive; do those need to be backed up?" the answer is a resounding **yes**. Just because the files are stored in the cloud doesn't mean that you won't lose them; you may just lose them for different reasons.

Yes, the service provider is most likely backing up its servers, but that does you no good if you accidentally delete a file—or worse, your online account gets hacked and the hacker deletes everything.

You must back up the data you keep in any online service, or you are at risk of losing all of it in an instant.

Be careful what files you place in the cloud, and how

The answer to "Can I use OneDrive space as my external hard drive for backups of my other files?" is a qualified "yes."

Cloud services are, in fact, great places to back up many files on your computer. In one operation, you get both backups (an additional copy of your data) and off-site backups (copies stored somewhere other than where your computer is located). That's a very good use of cloud storage as cloud backup.

However, there's a catch.

If your online account is compromised, it's possible your files can become accessible to hackers or others. As I'll discuss in a moment, that means the security of your online account is critical. It also means you may want to think twice about what files you place in the cloud.

Or you might want to consider how you place them there.

One alternative that works well is to make sure the files you place in the cloud are encrypted before they're put there. You can do that yourself, manually, or consider using a tool like BoxCryptor[37] to encrypt your cloud backup automatically.

―――――――――――――

[37] https://askleo.com/5722

Keep backing up locally

Unless you have an *amazingly* fast internet connection, the cloud is not a viable solution for image backups of your computer.

However, complete image backups of your computer are key to being able to recover quickly from a variety of disasters. You need to keep doing them.

Why aren't cloud backups ready for image backups? It's simply an issue of size and time. Image backups are large—multiple, if not hundreds, of gigabytes. Even on a fast internet connection, it could take days or weeks to upload the backup to online storage. Often image backups are created and updated faster than they could be uploaded to a cloud service.

So while cloud backup using cloud storage can be a very convenient and helpful *addition* to an overall backup strategy, it's in no way a replacement for local backups, nor is it an appropriate place to put your image backups.

Secure that account

The security of any online account is important, but it becomes even more important for the account you use for cloud backup.

It's too easy not to take your online account security seriously.

For any account into which you place important information—not only cloud backup, but email accounts, photo-sharing accounts, social media, and others—it's critical that you use as many of the techniques at your disposal to keep it as secure as you can manage. That includes:

- Using strong passwords[38]
- Using a different password[39] for every site or service
- Consider adding two-factor authentication
- Never sharing passwords with anyone
- Never logging into your account on a computer you don't completely trust
- Knowing when and how to use public internet connections and open Wi-Fi[40] safely
- Using common sense[41] to avoid malware, phishing attempts, and more[42]

You get the idea. It's basic internet security that we should all be doing anyway, but it's easy to overlook and easy to get wrong.

And when it comes to those important accounts, like an account you use for cloud backup, then additional measures—like perhaps two-factor authentication—might also be called for.

---

[38] https://askleo.com/4844
[39] https://askleo.com/11788
[40] https://askleo.com/4790
[41] https://askleo.com/16473
[42] https://askleo.com/2374

Part 3: Protect Your Computer

Protecting with Firewalls

Do I Need a Firewall, and If So, What Kind?

> **"**
> *I keep hearing about "firewalls" for my computer and that there are different types. Do I need one? If I do, what kind of firewall do I need?*

Yes. You need a firewall.

It's simply too risky to let your computer sit "naked" on the internet unless you really know what you're doing.

The good news is, you probably already have one and don't need to do a thing. Heck, you probably have two. But you should make sure.

What's a firewall?

Firewalls defend against a class of network-based threat constantly (yes, *constantly*) attempting to attack your computer. Those threats are stopped cold by a firewall.

And there's a good chance you already have one. Possibly even two.

In your car, a firewall is the "wall" of metal between you and the engine. Its purpose is to prevent engine fires from reaching you.

A firewall for your computer is much the same, except that the engine—the network you're connected to—is *always* on fire. The point of a firewall is to keep you from getting burned.

Network-based threats

A firewall protects your computer from network-based threats.

Almost all computers on the internet are under constant attack. Malware on other machines, hackers, botnets, and more are waging a slow but extremely persistent war, probing the internet to find unprotected vulnerabilities on other internet-connected computers. If they find such a vulnerability, they infect the machine they've found, or worse.

The basic concept of a firewall is very simple: it blocks or filters certain types of network traffic from ever reaching your computer.

Traffic that you want to reach your computer:
- Websites pages you visit
- Software you download
- Music or videos you might watch
- And more

Other traffic you definitely don't want:

- Your neighbor's machine, infected with a botnet, trying to connect to your machine over the network to spread the infection.
- Overseas hackers trying to gain entry to your machine over the network to steal your personal information.
- And more.

A firewall knows the difference.

If you look at the sets of examples above, they differ in one important aspect:
- Things you *want* are connections *you or your computer initiate*. At your request, your computer reaches out and asks for the webpages you visit, the software you download, or the music you listen to.
- Things that you *don't want* are connections from outside trying to come in without being invited.

That's an easy distinction for a firewall to make.

Two types of firewalls

Hardware firewalls

A router sitting between your computer and the internet is perhaps the best and most cost-effective firewall you can have. It's a piece of equipment[43] connected to both your computer and your internet service.

The router's job is to "route" data between your computer(s) and the internet. It also allows you to share an internet connection among many devices.

Routers watch for connections initiated by your computer reaching out to resources on the internet. When a connection is made, it keeps track, so when a response comes back, it knows which of your local machines gets the data.

The beneficial side effect is, if an outside computer tries to start a connection, the router doesn't know which computer to send it to. All it can do is ignore the attempt. That effectively blocks everything on the internet from trying to start a connection to a machine on your local network.

That makes your router a powerful incoming firewall. Your router will not, however, filter outgoing traffic.

---

[43] It may be combined with a modem, which converts your internet connection's technology into an ethernet connection, and/or with a wireless access point, giving you Wi-Fi connectivity. Or these may be three separate devices.

Software firewalls

Software firewalls are programs your computer runs. They operate as close to the network interface as possible, and monitor all your network traffic.

If you're not using a router and are connected directly to the internet, all of the network traffic will still technically reach your machine, but the firewall prevents malicious traffic from getting any further. Much like a router, a software firewall prevents the rest of your system from even realizing there is any malicious traffic.

In addition, some software firewalls can be configured to monitor outgoing traffic. If your machine becomes infected and malware attempts to "phone home" by connecting to a malicious site, or tries to infect other machines on your network, a software firewall can warn you and block the attempt.

Windows 10[44] has a built-in software firewall. It is turned on by default.

The Windows firewall is primarily an incoming-only firewall.

Choosing and setting up a firewall

I recommend using a router as your firewall. Since it's very likely you already have one, you're done.

There is disagreement. Some believe an outgoing firewall is important.[45] My position is, an outgoing firewall doesn't really protect; it notifies after something bad has already happened.

Routers are common, and a requirement for anyone who has more than one device sharing an internet connection -- which is all of us.

Software firewalls do make sense in a very important situation: they're one solution when you can't trust other computers on your local network. Don't trust the kids' ability[46] to keep their computer safe on the internet? Enable the software firewall on your computer. Heading out to the local open WiFi hotspot? Turn on the software firewall before you connect.

If you're running a reasonably current version of Windows, the firewall is probably on, and it's fine to leave it on all the time, even if you're behind a router. It has little impact and saves you from remembering to turn it on when you travel or have not-so-trustworthy guest on your network.

That's why I said earlier you might have two firewalls already: your router and your Windows firewall. And that's quite OK.

What firewalls can't do

It's important to remember that a firewall can't protect you from everything.

---

[44] And Windows 7, and 8, and 8.1. I believe in Vista and prior you needed to enable the firewall yourself.
[45] https://askleo.com/is_an_outbound_firewall_needed/
[46] https://askleo.com/protect-computers-local-network/

A firewall protects you from threats that arrive via malicious connection attempts from elsewhere on the internet.

A firewall will *not* protect you from things that you invite onto your machine yourself, such as email, attachments, downloads, and removable hard drives.

Nonetheless, protection from network attacks remains critically important.

Is an Outbound Firewall Needed?

> *Isn't an outbound firewall really important in many situations? I deliberately installed a free version of a key logger on my system and ran thorough scans through my anti-virus and anti-spyware programs. But the running key logger wasn't detected even though the key logger icon was right there in the system tray.*

A firewall with outbound detection can be of use, but you've captured my thoughts already: if it detects something, in a way it's already too late: your machine is infected.

Let's review what outbound firewalls are, why I rarely recommend them, and perhaps why your keylogger wasn't detected.

Firewalls

Firewalls protect you from certain classes of bad things out on the internet. The primary function of a firewall is to monitor traffic coming from the internet (inbound) and prevent bad stuff from reaching or affecting your computer.

Its job is to protect you from "them", where "them" means the bad guys on the internet.

My article Do I need a firewall, and if so, what kind?[47] has a good overview of firewalls in general, how they do what they do, and my recommended approach.

To summarize: my preference is to use a hardware device, such as a router with NAT (Network Address Translation) enabled. This does an incredibly effective job of hiding your computer from outside access. You can connect out, but outside computers cannot initiate a connection without you having explicitly configured your router to allow it.

Using a router also takes the burden of that work off your computer. In fact, a single router can act as a single effective inbound firewall for all computers connected behind it.

Outbound firewall

A traditional firewall monitors traffic heading toward your computer from the internet. An outbound firewall does just the opposite: it looks for threats originating on your computer attempting to connect out to the internet.

In a sense, it's protecting "them" from you.

While it's very generous of you to protect everyone else from your computer, the real difference is that it should block and alert you when something suspicious is happening, so you can take corrective action.

---

[47] https://askleo.com/1911

Outbound firewall shortcomings

In my opinion, outbound firewalls have several shortcomings, both technical and conceptual.

It's too late

As you pointed out, when an outbound firewall detects something malicious, it's because your machine is already infected. Something in your inbound security failed, and your machine very likely has malware.

Of course, it's nice to be alerted, but your inbound defenses—firewall and anti-malware scanners—*should* have already either prevented or detected the problem. With adequate inbound protection, an outbound firewall is mostly redundant.

It's intrusive

Outbound firewalls are only practically available as a part of third-party software firewalls you install on your machine. That means these firewalls take up additional resources to do their job.

A router will give you the inbound protection you need without taking up any additional resources.

It's frequently wrong

I'd say that the most common complaints about outbound firewalls are that it throws warning messages that are either incomprehensible or overly frequent, and it doesn't give enough information to make an informed decision about what action to take, if any.

Frequently, they simply report an outbound connection attempt, with little or no information beyond the remote IP address.

They often generate warnings arising from totally legitimate processes on the machine, such as accessing the internet for things like software updates, or even just the current time and date.

With too many errors, indecipherable messages, and false positives, people tend to ignore all the warnings after a while, rendering the outbound firewall completely ineffective.

The case for an outbound firewall

Is there a case for an outgoing firewall at all?

Many experts will disagree with me and say they add a lot of value, and the issues I've raised are off target or overstated.

Yes, it can act as an additional warning system. If it's not too intrusive, it might even be relatively benign.

But I remain of the opinion that if an outgoing firewall is, in fact, adding value, it's because your incoming protection is inadequate. If you're going to focus additional energy and resources on security, I'd much rather you focus on preventative solutions, rather than solutions that only kick in after something has happened.

Detecting your keylogger

Now, about your keylogger.

If it's showing up in the system tray, I'm not sure I'd classify it as malware.

It's open about what it's doing and easily visible. A key logger isn't of itself necessarily malware—there are many legitimate uses for the technology. Since it's not behaving like malware, I'm not surprised it's not detected as malware.

It also may not be reaching out to the internet. It may be storing the keystrokes it logs locally, or it may simply delay its upload of your activity until it's collected a certain amount of data, or until some other time.

But let's assume you did get infected by a truly malicious keylogger—one that was attempting to hide and send all your keystrokes to some overseas hacker in real time.

Well, at the risk of repeating myself too many times: *it's too late*. Your machine has been compromised, and you can no longer trust it—*and that includes trusting your firewall*. Yes, your outbound firewall might block the transmission—or it might not. The malware could, in fact, include additional code to reconfigure your firewall to let the malware's communication through.

This is almost worse than having no outbound protection at all. With the outbound firewall, you might think you're protected when in fact you are not. Without an outbound firewall, you know, and you know to focus your efforts on inbound protection to avoid the problem in the first place.

I know that others will disagree with me, but I remain unconvinced, and outbound firewalls are not something I use personally or generally advise.

Eight Steps to a Secure Router

> " *I'd like to know how to clear the history of my Linksys router. I'd also like to know how I can make it more secure and protect it from hacking .*

The topic is an important one: how do you make sure you have a secure router? As your firewall, it's your first line of defense against malware trying to get at your computer from the internet.

You want to make sure there aren't big gaping holes. And sadly, very often and by default, there are.

Here are the most important steps to a more secure router.

My router versus your router

I have to start with a caveat: there are hundreds, if not thousands, of different routers. Different brands and different models with differing capabilities, power, and, of course, at differing cost.

Most importantly, they have different administration interfaces.

What that means is, I can't tell you exactly how to make changes to your router step-by-step. The concepts I'll cover apply to almost all consumer-grade routers, and I'll be using an old and popular LinkSys BEFSR81 router and LinkSys WAP54G access point as examples.

You'll need to "translate" the examples to the equivalent settings on your own router or access point. Make sure you have access to the documentation that came with your router, or locate the user's manual online.

Already we see a common difference: you may well have a single device that combines both the router and wireless access point. You probably refer to it as simply your "router". In reality, there are two separate devices—a router that deals with network access, and a wireless access point that provides your Wi-Fi connectivity—that happen to be housed in a single box. In my case, they're in separate boxes.

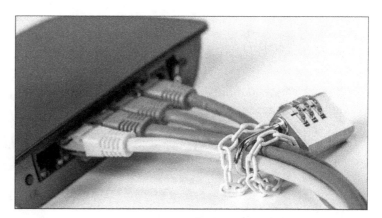

1. Change the default password

If you do nothing else to secure your router, *change the default password*. Change it to be something long and strong.[48] If your router supports it, a pass*phrase* of three or more words might be ideal.

---

[48] https://askleo.com/4844

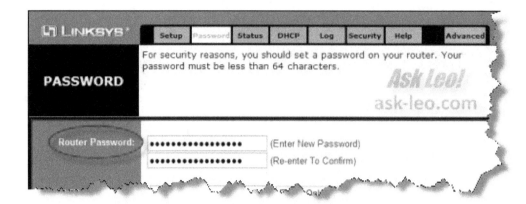

The reason for this is quite simple: it's a common gaping security hole.

For many years, almost every router and access point from the same manufacturer was shipped with the same default password. For LinkSys, if your login is a blank username and a password of "admin", as outlined in its manual, then *anyone and everyone knows it.* And anyone can log in to your router and undo any or all of the rest of the security steps we're about to take.

Then, any malware that takes advantage of the default passwords on routers can make changes without your knowledge.

Fortunately, in recent years, most—though not all—router manufacturers have been getting smarter. If the instructions that came with your router included checking a sticker on the actual router for the admin password, and that looks like a strong password, then the security hole is significantly smaller. Now only those people who can walk up to your router and look at that sticker can get in.

I'd change the password anyway.

2. Disable remote management

"Remote Management" is a feature that allows your router to be administered from anywhere out on the internet.

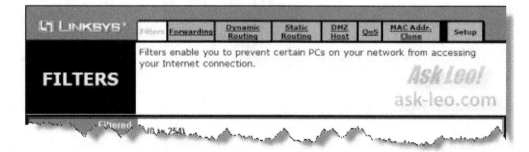

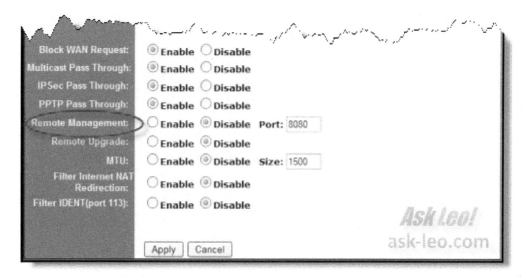

While this setting (coupled with a *very* strong password) might make sense for a handful of people,[49] for most folks there's absolutely no need to administer the router from anywhere but the local machines connected to it.

Make sure the remote management setting is off.

3. Turn off Universal Plug and Play

Universal Plug and Play (UPnP) is a technology that allows software running on your machine to configure services like port forwarding (a way of allowing computers outside your network to access your local computers directly) without you having to go in and administer the router manually.

It seems like a good idea, right?

Nope. Turn it off.

---

[49] Some ISPs will insist on this, but they'll also prevent you from administering your own router as well. More common is a scenario where you're responsible for supporting someone else's network – say that of a friend or family. Remote administration can be helpful in a case like that. Even so, I'd think twice about setting it up, and would insist on an exceptionally secure password if you do.

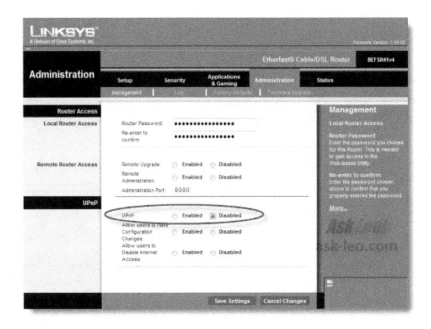

It turns out that malware can also be UPnP aware, and can make malicious changes to your router without your involvement or awareness.

(Note: UPnP is *unrelated* to Windows "Plug and Play" hardware detection; it's just another unfortunate collision of similar names.)

4. Add a WPA2 key

It's time for another password, this time to secure and encrypt your wireless connection.

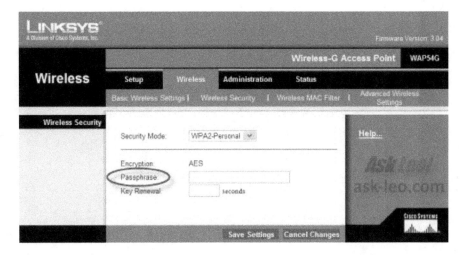

First, use **WPA2**, *not* WEP. WEP encryption turns out to be very easily crackable,[50] and even WPA (without the 2) has been shown to be vulnerable.

---

[50] It's essentially like having no encryption at all.

Second, just as you did for the router's administration password, select another good, secure key/password/passphrase (the terms are roughly interchangeable here). You only need to enter it once here and once on each machine allowed to connect to your wireless network.

Having a strong WPA2 key ensures that only machines you allow on your network can see your network, your traffic, and your router.

5. Disable WPS

WPS, or Wi-Fi Protected Setup, doesn't live up to its name—it's not very "protected" at all.

WPS was intended as a way to make setting up a protected Wi-Fi network easy. WPS would, with the push of a button, set up Wi-Fi encryption between the router and clients that supported it.

The problem with WPS is that the protocol is flawed in such a way that it is vulnerable to a brute force attack. A malicious entity within range can force their way onto your network, bypassing any encryption keys you might have set up.

WPS is enabled by default on many routers. Turn it off.

6. Turn off logging

This has less to do with configuring a secure router, and more to do with maintaining your privacy.

This is also about making sure logging is still turned off, since if a router supports any kind of logging at all, it'll likely be off by default.

Disable the logging, and no information will be kept on the router, or sent to any other machine. This should also clear any log the router has.

It's worth pointing out that most consumer-grade routers do not have the capacity to actually keep complete logs themselves. If they keep anything, it will only be a shorter, partial log. When enabled, some will offer to send the log to one of the computers on your network for storage. Simply disabling logging will not erase any logs stored elsewhere.

7. Secure your router physically

As we've already seen, even if the default administrative password is unique to your device, it's still visible to anyone with physical access to the router who can see the sticker on which it's printed.

In fact, your secure router may not be secure at all if anyone can just walk up to it.

All of your router's security settings can be reset in a flash if someone has physical access to the device. Almost all routers have a "reset to factory defaults" mechanism (typically by holding a reset button for a certain amount of time). If someone can walk up to your router and do that, all the security settings you've just enabled may be instantly erased.

Only you can judge whether or not you need this extra level of physical security, but make sure to consider it.

8. Check for firmware updates

Routers (and access points) are really just small computers dedicated to a single task: handling network traffic. Normally the software — referred to as "firmware" since it's stored within the device's hardware — is solid and just works.

Unfortunately, security vulnerabilities are sometimes discovered, requiring you to update your router's firmware to stay secure. This usually involves downloading a file for your specific router and using its administration interface to install the update. Some routers can fetch and install the update directly. Either way, the update is a manual step you need to take.

Checking to see if there's a firmware update for your router is also a manual step. Some routers perform the check at the push of a button in the administration interface. If not, you need to visit the manufacturer's support site, look for information pertaining to your specific model, and determine if a newer version of the firmware is available.

Two steps that aren't steps

Each time I mention this article, folks make two additional suggestions for Wi-Fi specifically that, do not improve security at all. In fact, they may harm security in some ways by providing a false sense of added security.

The first is MAC address filtering. I discuss this in more detail in Is MAC Address Filtering a Viable Wireless Security Option?,[51] but the bottom line is that like a cheap padlock, MAC address filtering only keeps out honest people. If someone wants to access your network MAC address filtering is easily bypassed.

The second suggestions is to turn off SSID broadcast on wireless networks. Even when not being broadcast, the SSID is still visible—unencrypted—in the packets of traffic sent to and from the router. Disabling the broadcast, does nothing to prevent someone with the skills from easily

---

[51] https://askleo.com/4350

discovering it. I discuss this in more detail in <u>Does Changing or Disabling the Broadcast of My Wireless SSID Make Me More Secure?</u>[52]

When it comes to Wi-Fi, putting a WPA2 password on the connection is currently your best security measure.

---

[52] https://askleo.com/5049

Protecting from Malware

What Security Software Do You Recommend?

> **"**
> *What security software should I use? What anti-virus is the best? How about a firewall? And what about spyware? Should I use one of the all-in-one packages that claim to do everything? Is there anything else I need?*

As you might imagine, I get questions like this all the time. As a result, I do have recommendations for security software and techniques to stay safe in various articles all over *Ask Leo!*

To make your life a little easier, here's a short version that sums it all up into four steps.

The short-short version

- Windows Security, in Windows 10, is my recommended anti-malware tool for most.
- Your router can serve as your primary firewall at home or work.
- Leave the Windows Firewall enabled as well, unless it causes problems.
- Let Windows Update keep your computer as up to date as possible.

That's it. Good basic protection in four steps. That's it.

Basic security software: Windows Security

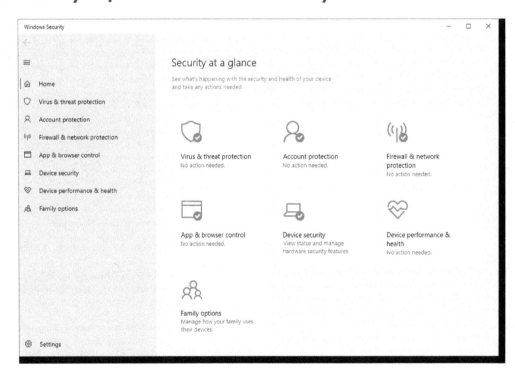

In Windows 10, Windows Security -- previously known as Windows Defender -- comes pre-installed. Microsoft seems to be improving it with every release.

Windows Security does a fine job of detecting malware without adversely impacting system performance or nagging you for renewals, upgrades, or up-sells. It just does its job quietly in the background -- exactly what you want from your anti-malware tool.

The ratings game

Every so often, Windows Security comes under fire for rating lower in tests published online than other security packages. I get push-back -- often angry push-back -- that it remains my primary recommendation.

There are several reasons I stick to that position.
- No anti-malware tool will stop all malware. Malware can and does slip by even today's highest-rated packages.
- "Highest-rated" changes depending on the date, the test, and who's doing the testing. There is no single clear, consistent winner.
- Regardless of how the data is presented, the differences among detection rates across most current anti-malware tools is relatively small compared to other factors.

There are also some practical reasons I continue to prefer Windows Security.
- It's free.
- It's already installed; there's nothing you need to do.
- It rarely impacts system performance.
- It keeps itself up to date using Windows Update.
- It has no hidden agenda -- it's not going to pester you with renewals, upgrades, or up-sells to tools you don't need.

It's not perfect, but no security tool is.

My recommendation stands. Windows Security remains a solid, free security package with minimal system impact. It should be appropriate for almost everyone.

Alternative security software and additions

On the other hand, I fully recognize that Windows Security might not be the right solution for everyone. No single product is.

This is where I run into some difficulty trying to make recommendations. The landscape keeps changing. Tools that were once clearly free have, on more than one occasion, moved to promoting their paid product so heavily that the free version virtually disappears. People download and install programs thinking they are truly free only to discover, instead, a free trial, or a free download (if you want to keep it past a certain length of time, you're required to purchase it).

Some programs have become as much self-promotion tools as they are anti-malware tools, bombarding you with sales pitches and upgrade offers to the point of getting in the way of your work.

Things keep changing. So to the extent that I mention specific tools below, *caveat emptor*: "let the buyer beware". I can't honestly predict that the tools will remain recommendation-worthy.

Malwarebytes Anti-Malware[53] has evolved over the years into a full-featured security package. It continues to have a good track record for removing troublesome malware other packages sometimes miss. (And yes, there remains a free version: after the "trial" of their pro version ends, what remains is the free version. The free version is an on-demand scanner only.)

AVG,[54] **Avira**,[55] and ~~Avast~~,[56] or the "three AV's", as I like to call them, are three other free solutions I've recommended over the years. I continue to hear both good things, and not so good things, about each, often in waves as each make significant updates.

Other name brand, but potentially not free, solutions include Kaspersky,[57] McAfee,[58] WebRoot,[59] and BitDefender[60]. [61]

Caveats with all

I need to reiterate some important points.
- Beware of "free". In most cases, a "free trial" is just that: a trial of a full-featured product eventually requiring payment. In some cases, like MalwareBytes, the "free trial" becomes a truly free version after the trial ends. In other cases, they are two separate downloads. And in other cases, there is no truly free version at all. Be sure you know which you are getting.

---

[53] https://www.malwarebytes.com/mwb-download/
[54] https://go.askleo.com/avg
[55] https://go.askleo.com/avira
[56] Or perhaps not: The Cost of Avast's Free Antivirus: Companies Can Spy on Your Clicks (https://www.pcmag.com/news/the-cost-of-avasts-free-antivirus-companies-can-spy-on-your-clicks, PCMag, January 2020)
[57] https://go.askleo.com/kaspersky
[58] https://go.askleo.com/mcafee
[59] https://www.webroot.com/
[60] https://go.askleo.com/bitdefender
[61] To be clear, I've not run any of the paid versions, and I've not run the "three AVs" in many years. Their mention here is simply based on their reputation over the years.

- Regardless of which you download, you are still likely to be faced with upgrade and up-sell offers, or even an ongoing subscription. Unless or until you know you want this, decline.
- Speaking of declining: when installing any of these, always choose custom installation, never the default. The default may include other unrelated software you don't need or want. Consider using Ninite[62] to install the free tools -- all are available there.

What else besides security software?

Firewall

For home and business use, I recommend the use of any good NAT router as a firewall. You probably already have one.

They don't have to be expensive, and are one of the simplest approaches to keeping your computer safe from network-based threats. If all the computers on the local network side of the router can be trusted, there's no need for an additional software firewall.[63]

When traveling, or if you don't trust the kids' computer connected to the same network as your own, I recommend turning on the built-in Windows Firewall. In recent versions of Windows, it's already on by default. There's no harm in leaving it on, but it can occasionally get in the way of some local machine-to-machine activities, like sharing files and folders.

Back up

I *strongly* recommend you back up regularly.

In fact, I can't stress this enough. 99% of the disasters I hear about could be *completely* avoided simply by having up-to-date backups.

Macrium Reflect[64] and EaseUS Todo[65] are the backup tools I currently use and recommend. More on backing up here: How Do I Back Up My Computer?[66]

Stay up to date

Keep your computer -- Windows *and* all the applications you run -- as up to date as possible.

In Windows 10, this happens automatically, as long as you don't take steps to disable it. Needless to say, I strongly recommend you not take those steps, and let Windows Update keep your system as up to date.

Many of the security issues we hear about are due to individuals (and, sadly, corporations) who have not kept their operating system or applications current with the latest available patches.

---

[62] https://askleo.com/21355
[63] https://askleo.com/3484
[64] https://askleo.com/4996
[65] http://todo.askleo.com/
[66] https://askleo.com/6643

And finally, Internet Safety: 7 Steps to Keeping Your Computer Safe on the Internet[67] has even more tips for keeping your computer safe.

---

[67] https://askleo.com/2374

Why Did My Security Software Not Detect a Virus on My PC?

> **"**
> *Why would an exploit not be caught or detected by my antivirus program (Avast) or Malwarebytes (running in the background)? If not detectable, how much "damage" can the exploit actually do if users follow prudent operating precautions? Would System Restore be usable if infected? I have also followed your advice and routinely image my Dell laptop.*

The question is a very good one: how can malware get past anti-malware programs to infect the software installed on your machine?

And more importantly, what can you do to protect yourself?

Let's define some terms with what I'm thinking is my silliest metaphor ever, and then talk about how to stay safe.

Vulnerabilities and Exploits

A *vulnerability* in software isn't a bad thing in and of itself. It's kind of like a hole in a bathroom wall: as long as no one's looking through the hole, there's no damage done.

Naturally, you'd like to have the problem fixed and the hole repaired (i.e. you'd like your software to be updated and the vulnerability removed), but as long as the hole hasn't been found by anyone, it's not really putting you at imminent risk. It shouldn't be there, of course, but as long as no one knows about it, all is well.

An *exploit* is like someone finding the hole and looking in at whatever's happening in your bathroom. If the hole is big enough, perhaps they can even reach in and steal personal things like your toothbrush, or flush your toilet when you're not looking.

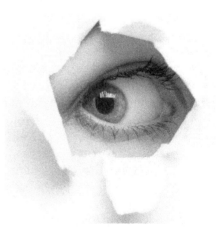

A software exploit could do things like look at the information on your computer, steal personal things like your passwords, or use your computer to send spam when you're not looking.

And yes, I just compared spam to whatever you might flush down your toilet.

Anti-malware tools

Now to factor in anti-malware tools.

The term *anti-malware* is really a catch-all for a couple of different types of security tools: anti-spyware and anti-virus (though the distinction is getting blurrier by the day).

- *Anti-spyware* tools are kind of like security cops. They don't know about the holes, but they have a list of all the *other* places from which you could be spied on. They monitor the doors and windows and make sure no one has installed a video camera in the medicine cabinet. As soon as they see suspicious activity in those locations, they alert you and attempt to remove the threat.

- *Anti-virus* tools are more like security cops with a big book of mug shots of all the people who are known to look in holes in bathroom walls. As soon as they see someone from that book, they kick them out, or at least let you know they're lurking about.

The problem, of course, is that these cops are only as good as the information they carry. If the anti-spyware cop is unaware of the fact that video cameras can also be placed in the light fixture, they won't check that. If the anti-virus cop doesn't have the photo of the Peeping Tom discovered elsewhere this morning, he won't recognize him.

That's why I so often insist that you not only have up-to-date anti-malware software (cops who know all the important tricks of the trade), but that you also make sure to update their databases of malware (the list of places to look and malcontents to look for) consistently.

The metaphor can be extended even further. Not all cops are the same; some are better at seeing certain kinds of things that others, others get better data from their head office, and so on.

And some are just incompetent.

Ultimately, though, not having up-to-date tools with up-to-date information is one way that malware makes it into your system.

Finding Holes

Unlike a bathroom wall, the vulnerabilities (or "holes") in software are often not obvious or easy to discover. It's not uncommon for a vulnerability to exist for years before someone stumbles across it and develops a way to exploit it.

To continue the "computer software is like a bathroom" story even further, the holes in your wall are very, very difficult to find. Depending on the quality of the original builder, there may be easier-to-find holes, but those are often found and fixed relatively quickly.

And here's the scary part: hackers are like someone who spends all day and night looking at your bathroom wall from the outside, hoping to find a hole no one else has found before. It's not a new hole—it was there all along—but it is a new discovery, and often termed a new vulnerability.

Or sometimes they'll find a new way to use a previously known hole that hasn't been patched yet.

Either way, as soon as they're successful, they create malware to exploits the fact that your bathroom wall (the software on your computer) has an unpatched hole.

Fixing Holes

"So just plug the holes!" I hear you yelling.

Exactly. The problem is, as I mentioned above, the holes can be *extremely* hard to find.

But once they're found, the hole is patched by updating the software on your machine to versions that no longer have the holes.

Usually. Some holes are fixed more quickly than others, and some may not be fixed at all. Some holes are harder to patch than others.

And some holes are worse than others. A hole that allows someone to see your toothbrush might be less important than a hole that allows someone to actually steal it.

Another issue is that fixing a hole can damage the wall, sometimes to the extent that a new hole is created elsewhere. By that, I mean fixing a bug in software can unintentionally introduces other bugs. Thus the benefit of fixing a known hole has to be weighed against the risk that doing so might create another hole we won't know about.

The bottom line here, though, is that having out-of-date software—software with known holes in it that have been fixed by updates you haven't downloaded yet—is another way malware can find its way onto your machine.

Avoiding holes: extreme version

An experience with Java a few years ago is a great example of a widespread and newly discovered vulnerability.

To continue our now tortured comparison:
- Many, many people had this model of "bathroom". (Many people had Java installed.)
- Many holes were found and repaired in this bathroom's walls. (Java has a history of vulnerabilities.)
- A new hole was discovered and new people were found looking in, before the security cop's mug book could be updated. (A new "zero day" exploit of a vulnerability in Java was found in the wild.)
- Until the hole was patched, everyone using this bathroom was vulnerable to having their toothbrush stolen, or worse. (Everyone with Java on their machine was at risk.)

The common advice was to remove the bathroom completely (uninstall Java), use a different bathroom (use alternate tools that don't use Java), or avoid using a bathroom altogether (don't do whatever it was you were doing that required Java).

The metaphor breaks down at this point, because while most of us may not need Java (the advice remains to uninstall it unless you know you need it), we all need to use the bathroom.

Avoiding holes: more common version

The advice for avoiding software exploits is the same as it's always been:
- Keep your computer software up to date. (Keeps the holes we know about patched.)
- Keep your anti-malware tools up to date, and keep their databases up to date. (Keep the security cops sharp and equip them with current information of what to look for.)
- In some cases, uninstall software that is known to have issues. (Keeps you from doing things that a Peeping Tom might see or use against you.)

- And of course, don't invite a crowd of Peeping Toms onto your computer by opening attachments you're not certain are safe, running questionable downloads, or visiting questionable sites.

In other words, keep your bathroom clean and don't invite strangers in.

And, yes, even after doing all that, there's still the possibility of a hole you don't know about being found and exploited before all the defenses are updated.

If infected...

What can malware do? Essentially, anything it wants. Naturally, the specifics depend on the size of the hole being exploited and what's available on your computer, but it's safest to assume that once a vulnerability on your machine is exploited and an infection occurs, all bets are off.

That's one reason that I so strongly recommend regular backups. If your machine is infected today, restore to yesterday's backup, and the infection is gone. Period.[68]

System Restore can sometimes help, but there are two problems with it:
- In my experience, it's extremely unreliable. There's nothing worse than counting on System Restore to save you, only to have it respond with things like "No restore points found" or the like.
- You're still not sure the malware is gone. System Restore doesn't restore everything, and those things it does not restore remain infected if they were, in fact, infected to begin with.

Try System Restore if you like—be sure to run full and updated anti-malware scans thereafter—but it's not something I feel at all confident relying on.

As for me ... I'm moving my toothbrush. :-)

---

[68] This is where the metaphor *really* breaks down. I mean, who keeps a daily backup of their bathroom? ☺

How Do I Remove Malware from Windows 10?

One question that shows up almost every day in the Ask Leo! inbox is how to remove malware.

Every day.

The scenarios differ, but the problem is the same: a machine has been infected with spyware, a virus, ransomware, or some other form of malware, and that machine's owner is having a tough time getting rid of it.

Often, anti-malware software is installed that "should" have taken care of it before it got to this stage.

Hopefully, that will never be you.

Let's review the steps I recommend for removing malware *and* reducing the chances it'll happen again.

A word about prevention

If there's one thing I would have you take away from this article, it would be this:

Prevention is much less painful than the cure.

As we'll see in a moment, the steps to remove malware can be painful and time consuming. Knowing how to stay safe on the internet[69] is much, much easier in comparison.

So, let's look at what to do when prevention has failed.

Back up

My strong recommendation is that you start by taking a complete image backup of your system.

Why would you want to back up a system you *know* is infected with malware?

A backup taken now is an "it-can't-get-any-worse-than-this" fallback. Some of the techniques we use to remove malware run the risk of breaking things and making the situation worse. With this backup at the ready, you can always restore and start over with nothing lost.

---

[69] https://askleo.com/2374

Restore a prior backup

If you've been taking regular backups, restoring a prior one is often the most expedient step, and can save a lot of time and energy.

Simply restore your machine completely from the most recent full system backup, plus any incremental backups (often handled transparently by your backup software) taken before the infection occurred.

Except for learning from the experience, you're done.

Unfortunately, most people don't have this option available to them. Most people don't begin backing up until after they've experienced data loss or a severe malware infection. One of the lessons they learn is that a recent backup can save them from almost any problem—including malware.

Update the anti-malware database

If you have anti-malware software installed, make sure it's up-to-date. This includes more than just the software itself: *the database of malware definitions* must also be current.

Almost all anti-malware tools use databases of malware definitions. They change daily, if not more often, and as a result need to be updated regularly.

Many programs will do this automatically, but if for some reason they do not, the program will not "know" about the most recent forms of malware. Make sure the database is up-to-date so yours does.

Perform a full scan

Quite often, anti-malware tools regularly perform a "quick" or fast scan. That's typically sufficient for day-to-day operations.

But not today.

Fire up your anti-malware tools and run a full/advanced/complete scan of your entire system drive. If you have a single tool, that might be one run; if you use multiple tools, such as separate anti-virus and anti-spyware tools, then run a full scan with each. This may take some time, but let the tools do their job.

This also applies if your anti-malware automated scans have stopped working for some reason (that reason often being malware). If this full scan discovers something, it might be worth checking to make sure the security software is properly configured to scan automatically as well.

Try another anti-malware tool

No anti-malware tool catches all malware.

I'll say it again: *there is no single tool that will catch every single piece of malware out there.* None. Some are better than others, some catch more than others, but none of them catch everything.

So trying additional reputable tools is a reasonable approach.

I recommend the free version of Malwarebytes' Anti-Malware[70] as the first tool to use. It has a reputation for removing some nasties other tools apparently miss. Once again, run a full scan.

Regardless of which tool you select, *stick with reputable tools.* When a machine is infected, most people tend to panic and download just about anything and everything that claims to be an anti-malware tool. *Don't do that.* There are many less-than-reputable individuals out there ready to take advantage of your panic.

Do some research before downloading anything, or you may just make the problem worse instead of better.

Research specific removal instructions

If your anti-malware software tells you the *name* of the specific malware you're dealing with, that's good information—even if it can't remove it.

Search for that malware, and you're likely to find specific removal instructions at one or more of the major anti-malware vendor sites. These instructions can be somewhat technical and intimidating, so take your time to follow them precisely, or get a techie friend to help.

Those instructions often come with offers to remove the malware—for a price. As long as it's an *option* (in other words, the manual removal instructions are also provided), then it may be a viable alternative if the company is one you trust. On the other hand, if all you're presented with is a promise and a price, move on.

Some sites offer free tools you can download to remove specific malware. Once again, *use caution.* When the tools are from reputable sources, they're a quick way to avoid some hassle. When the tools are really just more malware in disguise, they'll make your problems worse.

If you download anything to help address the problem, make sure that wherever it comes from, it's an organization you know and trust.[71]

---

[70] https://askleo.com/5765
[71] https://askleo.com/24333

Surrender

This is the only sure-fire way to remove any virus. 100%. Guaranteed.

In fact, it's the only way to know that you've removed a virus. Once infected, none of the steps above, *aside from restoring from a backup taken before the infection*, are guaranteed to remove the malware even if they report that things are clean. Once infected, all bets are off. An infection can fool anti-malware software into thinking that everything is fine even when it's not.

There's just no way to know.

The only way to be absolutely positive that you've removed any and all viruses is:

- **Back up**. If you haven't already, back up the entire system. You'll use this to restore your data after we're done.
- **Reformat**. Reformatting erases the entire hard disk of everything: the operating system, your programs, your data, and most important of all, any and all viruses and malware. This may be part of the next step, as most Windows set-up programs offer to reformat the hard drive before installing Windows.
- **Reinstall**. Yes, reinstall everything from scratch. Reinstall the operating system from your original installation media. (Or restore the system to an image backup you took when you got the machine, which preserved the "factory original" state.) Reinstall applications from their original media, downloads saved elsewhere, or recovered from your backup.
- **Update**. Update everything, in particular making sure to bring Windows as completely up-to-date as possible for the most current protections against all known and patched vulnerabilities. Applications, particularly your anti-malware tools, should be updated as well.
- **Restore**. Restore your data by carefully copying it from the backups you created when we started. By "carefully," I mean take care to only copy the data you need, so as not to copy back the malware—don't copy potential sources of infection. It's true there is no guarantee you won't copy the malware back, so copy only what's absolutely needed, and make sure your anti-malware tools are running and up-to-date.
- **Learn**. Take stock of how this happened, what you might have done to get infected in the first place, and what might have helped you recover more efficiently. Consider instituting a frequent system backup.

It's not your fault, but it is your responsibility

By now, I hope you can see why prevention is so *much* less painful than the cure.

Taking a few extra steps to keep things up-to-date, avoiding those cute virus-laden downloads and attachments, and learning how to stay safe is much easier than the recovery process I've just outlined.

And having backups can make the recovery process as close to painless as possible if you do get infected.

Yes, it's not your fault. But *it is your responsibility* to learn the basics about staying safe when you use your computer.

In an ideal world, we'd never have to worry about malware, or the "bad guys" trying to fool us into doing things we really shouldn't. But you already know this isn't an ideal world; software isn't perfect and never will be. There will always be someone out to scam the vulnerable.

Even though it's not your fault, you still need to be the one to get educated and take the steps needed to stay safe.

Right or wrong, it's just a practical reality.

How Do I Remove Malware that Blocks Downloads?

> " *I am trying to fix a computer that has malware preventing me from getting into regedit and Task Manager. It will not let me boot into safe mode. It will not let me install any anti-spyware or anti-virus software. I'm not sure where to go from here. It has stopped me from doing much of anything to get the malware off the computer. Any suggestions?*

Sadly, this is all too common. Malware can be pretty sophisticated, and it can work hard to prevent you from removing it. That means you may be blocked from downloading or running anti-malware software, or be prevented from running tools already on your machine that might help.

I'll save the "prevention is so much easier than the cure" missive for a moment. We just want this fixed.

There are things that we can try, but unfortunately, there are no guarantees.

The problem: when malware interferes

What you're seeing is the malware on your machine actively watching for you to try to remove it[72] and thwarting your attempts.

It's watching for downloads that "look like" anti-malware tools, and web (or other) access that might be going to anti-malware sites. It's even monitoring what programs you run. When it sees you doing anything that could lead to its removal, it steps in to either redirect you to sites of its choosing, or simply cause the operation to fail.

We'd love to download and run anti-malware tools, but we can't.

So we have to get creative.

Run Windows Defender Offline

I recommend that you begin by running an offline malware scan. In previous versions of Windows, this involved downloading and running Windows Defender Offline,[73] but it's built in to Windows Security in Windows 10.[74]

Click the Start button and search for "offline scan". Click on **Virus & threat protection** when it

---

[72] https://askleo.com/3811

[73] https://askleo.com/5974

[74] As of this writing, many people are reporting issues with Windows Defender Offline being unable to update its malware database, and in turn being able to actually run. I'm retaining this as my go-to recommendation in the hopes that Microsoft will soon fix the error. This article on Windows Defender Offline also includes alternative tools you can use that work similarly.

appears. Click on Scan options, select "Microsoft Defender Offline scan", and finally click **Scan now**.

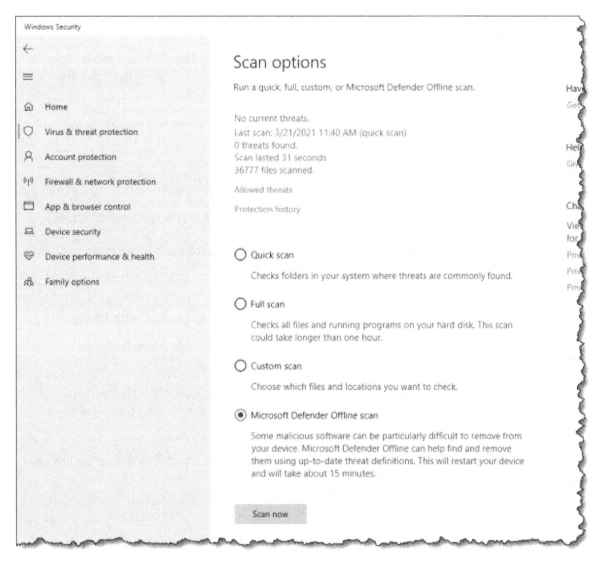

Your computer will reboot and run Microsoft Defender Offline.

Let the tool perform a thorough scan of your machine. Hopefully, it will detect and remove the malware that's causing your problem.

If it doesn't detect and remove it, or if you can't run Windows Defender Offline, or if you just want to keep scouring your machine with additional tools, there are other tactics.

Temporarily kill the malware

One possible solution to the blocking problem is to temporarily kill the malware. This won't remove it, but it may allow you to download tools that will.

The folks at BleepingComputer.com[75] have created a tool called RKill[76] that does exactly that.[77] You may need to download RKill on another machine (because it may be blocked on the infected machine), but you can copy it over to your machine using a USB drive or something else.

You may also need to rename Rkill.exe to something else (like "notRkill.exe" or "leo.exe"). Once again, the malware may be paying attention to the name of every program being run, and may prevent the software from running if it recognizes the name.

Run the program, and *do not reboot*. Rebooting will "undo" the effect of having run RKill. Any malware RKill killed will return if you reboot.

Download and run Malwarebytes Anti-Malware

With the malware temporarily killed, you may be able to download and run anti-malware tools.

Malwarebytes Anti-Malware[78] is currently one of the most successful tools at identifying and removing the types of malware that we're talking about here.

Download the free version, install and run it, and see what it turns up. Once again, you may need to download the tool on another machine and copy the download over, as you did with RKill.

Try other tools

After running RKill, you may (or may not) be able to run some of the other tools the malware was blocking. You can try your already-installed anti-malware tools, registry-editing tools, Task Manager, Process Explorer, and others.

You can also try your other anti-malware tools. Either they will be able to download an update that catches this problem, or you can download another tool that will.

But in general, my money is on Malwarebytes.

What if nothing works?

If none of what I've discussed so far works, then things get complicated.

You may consider these options:
- Boot from another bootable antivirus rescue CD. There are several, including from several anti-virus vendors. If you have a favorite anti-malware vendor, check with them to see if they provide a bootable scanning solution. These are interesting because they boot from the CD or USB, not your hard drive. That means the malware doesn't have a chance to operate and block you. You can then run a scan of your hard disk, and hopefully clean it off.

---

[75] https://go.askleo.com/bleeping
[76] https://go.askleo.com/rkill
[77] Be careful. At times, ads immediately above the download link look like the actual link to download the software. They are not. Be sure to grab RKill itself.
[78] https://askleo.com/5765

- Remove the hard disk and place it in or connect it to another machine. Hardware issues aside, this needs to be done with care to prevent the malware from spreading. Just like booting from that CD, however, this boots from the other machine's installation, not yours. You can then run anti-malware tools against your drive and hopefully clean it off.

Restore from backup

One of the best—and often quickest—solutions is to restore your machine using a recent image back up.

Assuming you have one, of course.

Regular backups are *wonderful* for this. They return your machine to the state it was in prior to the malware infection. It's as if the infection never happened.

This is another reason why I harp on backing up so often.

It does have to be the correct type of backup: either a full-system or image backup. Simply backing up your data will not be helpful in a scenario like this unless you are forced to take the final solution (see below).

For the record, my opinion is that Window's System Restore is pretty useless[79] when it comes to malware infections (assuming System Restore hasn't already been completely disabled by the malware). Give it a try if you like, but I don't have much hope for its success.

The final solution

That subtitle sounds dire because it is.

As I've mentioned before,[80] once it's infected with malware, your machine is no longer yours. You have no idea what's been done to it. You also have no idea whether the cleaning steps you took removed any or all of the malware that was on the machine.

Even if it looks clean and acts clean, there's no way to prove it is clean.

You know it *was* infected, but there's no way to know that it's not now.

Scary, eh?

The only way for you to know with absolute certainty that the malware is gone is to reformat your machine and reinstall everything from scratch.

Sadly, it's often the most pragmatic approach to removing particularly stubborn malware. Sometimes, all of the machinations that we go through trying to clean up from a malware infection end up taking much more time than simply reformatting and reinstalling.

---

[79] https://askleo.com/5027
[80] https://askleo.com/3811

And reformatting and reinstalling is the only approach known to have a 100% success rate at malware removal.

If you don't have a backup of your data, then at least copy the data off somehow before you reformat. Boot from a Linux Live CD or DVD if you must (Ubuntu's a good choice). That'll give you access to all of the files on your machine and allow you to copy them to a USB device, or perhaps even upload them somewhere on the internet.

Aftermath

After things are cleared up and working again, take a few moments to consider how to prevent this from happening again, as well as what you can do to make the next time easier:

- See if you can identify how the infection occurred and then, to whatever extent you can, *never do that again.* ☺
- Make sure you have the most up-to-date security measures to stay safe on the internet.[81]
- Invest in a backup solution of some sort. Nothing can save you from more different kinds of problems than a regular backup.[82]

As I said at the beginning, prevention is much, much easier than the cure.

---

[81] https://askleo.com/2374
[82] https://askleo.com/6643

Will Using an On-Screen Keyboard Stop Keyloggers?

> **"**
> *Will using the on-screen keyboard in Windows stop keyloggers?*

The short answer is very simple: *no*.

I get a surprising amount of push-back on this, but the simple truth remains: while it might stop some, it's nothing you can count on to be 100% effective.

Keyloggers are a form of malware that record your keystrokes to capture things like your login usernames and passwords so hackers can get into your accounts. Let's look at the path of keystrokes from your finger to your computer to see the various ways your keystrokes can be intercepted and logged.

The keyboard connection

Typically, when you type a key on your keyboard, a microprocessor within it sends signals via the cable connecting it to your computer.

Here we encounter the very first point of vulnerability. No, not the microprocessor in the keyboard (technically possible, but exceptionally unlikely)—but the cable, or rather, what the cable plugs into.

Particularly lucrative targets are public computers, where someone comes along and installs a physical device between the computer and keyboard—a device that intercepts and logs every keystroke entered. Sometime later they come back, remove the device, and take with it all the information users of that computer entered.

As it turns out, wireless keyboards can be worse. Wireless keyboards actually *broadcast* the keystrokes you're typing. Any receiver within range can "listen in". Wireless keyboards do encrypt their data, so in theory, the information should be safe, but the quality of the encryption can vary based on the age of the keyboard and the vendor. In addition, the concept of "in range" turns out to be much further than most people think, particularly for a thief with equipment dedicated and tuned to this purpose.

The good news is that your on-screen keyboard *does* protect you against these two specific types of keyboard-related threats. By using the on-screen keyboard, you're bypassing those components of the keyboard hardware that could be compromised.

The bad news is that hardware-based keyloggers are rare. Much more common are software-based threats.

The keyboard software

Once your keystrokes arrive at the computer from the keyboard, they are processed by a keyboard device driver which (to oversimplify) handles the translation of the keyboard "scan codes", as they're called, to the letters, numbers, and symbols Windows applications expect.

Keyloggers typically insert themselves into the receiving end of this process: they get the keystrokes from the keyboard as they are passed on to Windows.

This is where the on-screen keyboard scenario gets interesting.

The on-screen keyboard application is a "virtual" keyboard. It has its own device driver, which, to Windows, "looks like" a real keyboard.

As a result, the keystrokes it sends to Windows can *easily be captured* by the same key-logging software capturing keystrokes from the real keyboard, if that keylogger has installed itself in the proper place.

But it gets worse. Much worse, actually.

A keylogger is just malware

Perhaps the most important concept to remember here is that keyloggers are just another form of malware.

And malware can do *anything*; keylogging malware can actually capture much more than just keystrokes.

You use the virtual keyboard by using your mouse to point and carefully click at the image of a key on the keyboard. A keylogger could, then, for every mouse click:
- Capture the location of the mouse on the screen.
- Capture a screenshot image of the screen, or just the area "around" the mouse pointer.

The keylogger has captured a series of images showing exactly where you clicked and in what order. In other words, it's captured your virtual keystrokes.

Note that this approach to keylogging also bypasses one of the more common so-called security techniques of randomizing the keyboard layout on the screen. You still have to be able to see where to click, and the logger simply logs what you see and where you click, regardless of how the keyboard is laid out.

Keyloggers as threats

How big a threat is all this?

It depends on whom you ask. In my opinion, "normal" keyloggers—those that record only keystrokes—are a fairly common threat, and are one reason why anti-malware protection, general internet safety, and the use of common sense in general is so important. So yes, they're out there.

The real question is, how pervasive are these more sophisticated keyloggers, which do more than capture keyboard keystrokes, but use other techniques to effectively achieve the same result?

It's hard to say, but I have to say it again: keyloggers are "just" malware. If they're on your machine at all, you have a problem, and that problem may not be limited to logging what you type. Like any malware, you might not even realize they're there until it's too late. As a result, focusing on solutions targeted only at thwarting keyloggers is not only fundamentally misguided, but it also diverts your attention from a much bigger problem: if you have a keylogger, *you have malware.*

Focus on avoiding, or removing, malware of all sorts, and you'll be avoiding or removing keyloggers as a side effect.

And I would never rely on a virtual keyboard of any sort as some kind of security measure.

How Do I Remove PUPs and Other Unexpected Things From My Computer

Ending up with random software on your machine that you never wanted in the first place is annoying as all heck.

So-called PUPs (for Potentially Unwanted Programs, although there's rarely any "potentially" about it) are tools, settings, utilities, browser toolbars, extensions, and more software installed on your computer as a result of installing something else. PUPs are rarely even related to what you're installing.

I'll talk a little about prevention, but first, let's walk through the steps I recommend when you suddenly realize you've been saddled with software you didn't know you'd agreed to and certainly never wanted.

Start with a backup

The steps we are about to take have a small chance of causing problems.

Whenever that's the case, I strongly recommend you take a full image backup of your machine before you do anything else. That way, you'll have that backup to restore should anything below go wrong.

Uninstall the somewhat well-behaved PUPs

A number of unexpected toolbars and other applications that show up on your machine are "relatively" well behaved; by that I mean they are somewhat easy to uninstall using official mechanisms.

Start in the Windows Settings app, and click on **Apps**.

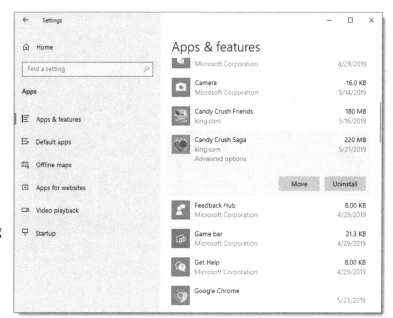

Look for the item by name. Sometimes that can be tricky, as applications are intentionally named obscurely to make them more difficult to remove, but the well-behaved items we're looking for here should be relatively clear. Look for names that include the word "toolbar", in particular, as those are some of the browser-behavior-altering pests that often put us in this scenario.

Right-click the item you want to uninstall, and click Uninstall.

We'll do the next steps even if it appeared to work, because in many cases there will be traces left over, and sometimes those traces can reinstall the PUP.

Run Malwarebytes

If you don't have it already, download and install the *free* version of Malwarebytes Anti-Malware.[83]

Important: The free version is, at first, a free trial of their paid version. It will nag you to register/upgrade/license the product. *You do not need to do so.* Simply use the product as described here. After a period of time (two weeks, at this writing) the trial will revert to the purely free version. It may continue to nag you, but it will keep working.

Run the program, if it hasn't started automatically, and click Scan to perform a scan.

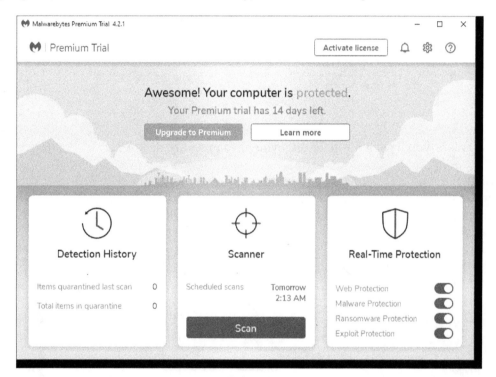

The Malwarebytes scan may take a while.

---

[83] http://www.malwarebytes.org/free/

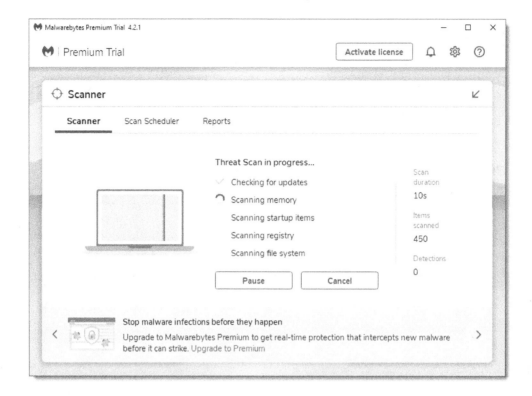

When it's complete, you'll get a notification if you have malware or PUPs.

Even if no actual malware is detected, potentially unwanted programs—PUPs—may still be found. Malwarebytes will show you the entire list. You can review the list if you like, but in general, the correct next step is to simply quarantine everything. You will likely need to reboot.

A clean scan is your goal.

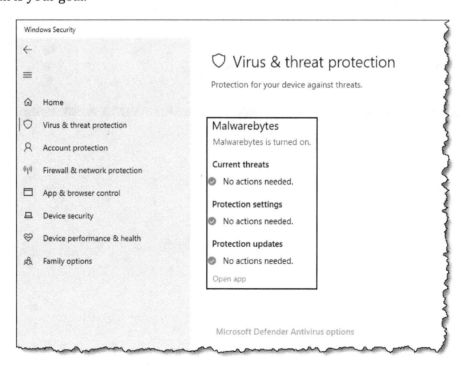

Note that you may want to uninstall Malwarebytes, as its trial version will have disabled Windows Defender in Windows Security. This isn't really a problem; you shouldn't have two real-time security solutions running at the same time, and Windows Security knows to step aside when Malwarebytes is installed. That being said, if you don't plan on keeping Malwarebytes, you'll probably want to remember to uninstall it when all is said and done. If you don't, after the trial period it will step aside; Windows Security will resume full real-time protection, and Malwarebytes will remain available for on-demand scans.

It's possible that Malwarebytes is unable to remove some PUPs. If that's the case (or even if it's not), I still want you to take one more step.

Run AdwCleaner

AdwCleaner is perhaps best downloaded from our friends over at BleepingComputer.com.[84] (AdwCleaner was purchased by Malwarebytes in 2016, but remains a separate tool.)

Speaking of being careful, remember to avoid advertisements that say "Download" or "Free Download." Those are *not* the programs you want. The button that I used simply read, "Download Now @BleepingComputer."

AdwCleaner has no install. Once downloaded, simply run it, and answer Yes to any UAC prompt.

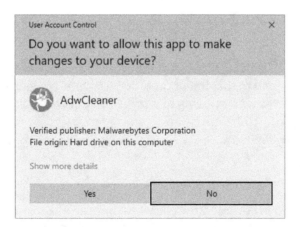

Also click I agree to any licensing terms agreement. Click Scan Now.

---

[84] https://go.askleo.com/adwcleaner

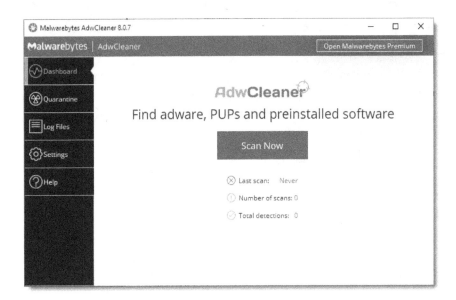

Once the scan is complete, AdwCleaner will present its scan results.

If you're not certain about what AdwCleaner finds, go ahead and let it clean up anything you don't recognize by clicking Clean & Repair. (It first warns you that all programs should be closed.)

The ultimate removal

Even with the tools I've outlined, and other tools that may also be used or may come along later, there's a real possibility that the unwanted software will *still* not be completely or successfully removed. This often happens when the PUP is new and the security-software makers are still catching up to the latest tricks it might be playing.

It's worthwhile to consider restoring to a recent backup image.[85] Restoring will make these things go away *every single time*.

If you have a back-up image of the machine as it was prior to these pests having been installed, you can simply restore your machine to that image, and they're gone. No fancy tools are needed, and you needn't just hope that it works. Restoring to a prior backup works *every time*.

Presuming, of course, you have one.

Prevention

PUPs and related pests arrive in several different ways, but the most common method is by being "offered" to you when you install something else. Often, the offer is hidden and defaulted to Yes. The technicality is that by choosing this default (or not unchecking the appropriate box) when you install some program you've downloaded, you're actually *asking* for this other software, these PUPs, to be installed.

Don't do that.

---

[85] https://askleo.com/6643

Whenever you install any software—*even software you've purchased*—always choose the "Custom" or "Detailed" option. Choose whatever option is *not* the default option.

Then pay very close attention to every option you're presented. If it offers you something that is not clearly related to the software you want, *uncheck it*. If it offers to change your search page, *uncheck it*. If it offers to install some toolbar, *uncheck it*.

You get the idea.

The bottom line is, if you're not careful when you install software—even software from reputable vendors—you may end up with things you never expected or wanted.

There's nothing "potentially unwanted" about it.

How Do I Avoid Ransomware? The 3 Things You're Hopefully Already Doing

> **"** *How can I prevent this new risk of criminals encrypting files on my hard drive and then demanding a ransom to unlock the data? Is having a router and software firewall enough?*

In other words, how do you avoid ransomware?

Let's look at ransomware—software that holds your computer hostage until you pay up—and how best to protect yourself.

Spoiler alert: you already know the answer.

What is ransomware?

Though it continues to get lots of press, ransomware is nothing new.

Ransomware is malware that encrypts files on your machine and then presents a message offering to decrypt and recover your files if you pay a ransom. Recent versions attacking businesses also threaten to release copies of sensitive data captured at the same time.

Most current variants use good encryption, so once you've fallen victim, the outlook can be pretty bleak.

But note the word I used: malware.

Please understand this: *ransomware is just malware.*

There's nothing special about ransomware and how it gets on your machine. It uses the same techniques as any other malware. Currently, it is most often distributed in email attachments or as downloads of some form.

Ransomware is very *destructive* malware, but it's just malware.

That should give you a huge clue on how to avoid it.

How to avoid ransomware

You avoid ransomware exactly the same way you avoid all viruses and malware.
- Run up-to-date anti-malware tools.[86] I happen to recommend Windows Defender, but there are many, many others. Make sure that they are running and up-to-date.

---

[86] https://askleo.com/3517

- Keep your system and software up-to-date.[87] Yes, this means letting Windows automatically update itself, as well as any applications that have self-updating capabilities.
- Use common sense.[88] Don't download random things from the internet, and don't open attachments you aren't *completely* certain are valid and correct.

In short, do all the things you should *already* be doing to keep yourself safe on the internet.[89]

More importantly, back up

If your machine does contract ransomware, having a recent backup[90] can save you almost immediately.

If you get ransomware on Tuesday, restoring to a backup taken on Monday makes it almost a non-event. Aside from any work performed since the Monday backup, you'd have your machine running again in no time, without paying any ransom.

There is almost *nothing* a good backup can't save you from. This is another case where even something as scary as ransomware doesn't need to get in your way.

Ransomware-specific protection

CryptoPrevent is a popular tool mentioned by many to avoid ransomware. Unfortunately, it doesn't prevent it.

Once installed, it prevents specific actions many variants of ransomware are known to use. (In rare cases, legitimate applications might require these same types of actions, but it's rare.)

Similarly, Windows 10 has added explicit ransomware protection to Windows Defender in the form of "Controlled folder access".

---

[87] https://askleo.com/21710
[88] https://askleo.com/16473
[89] https://askleo.com/2374
[90] Several people have expressed concern that a backup drive, if connected, may also be encrypted and held ransom. It can happen, but to me, it's much more important a drive remain connected so regular backups happen automatically. More here: Will Malware Infect the Backups on My Connected Backup Drives as Well?

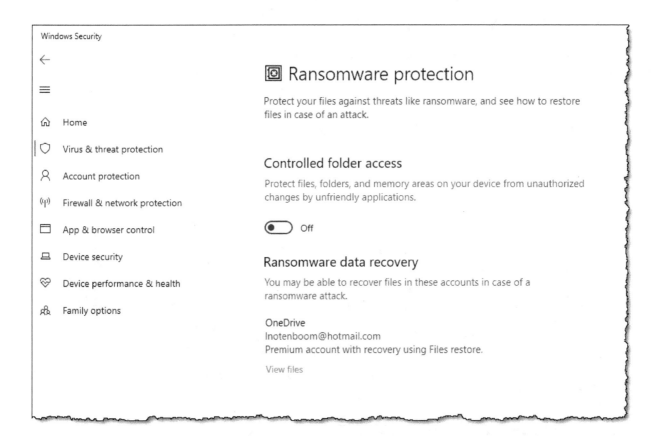

Similar to CryptoPrevent, some applications may have problems if this feature is enabled.

If installing CryptoPrevent or enabling Controlled Folder Access helps you feel safer and doesn't interfere with something else you need, by all means, feel free to enable them. They'll protect you from a lot, including some non-ransomware forms of malware. For the record, I use neither.[91]

My concern with both these approaches is that they focus exclusively on preventing the malware's malicious behavior, but *only after the malware has already infected your machine*. In other words, if they helped, it's because malware made it to your machine.

That's the problem to focus on. That's what I believe is most important to prioritize — preventing malware in the first place — and I don't want any tool or technique to give you a false sense of security leading to letting your guard down.

Should I pay the ransom?

No. Never.

Paying them just encourages them to keep doing this. Sadly enough, enough people do pay that it's apparently turning into quite a lucrative endeavor. Don't be one of those people.

Stay safe, back up, and never negotiate with hostage takers—even when it's your data they take.

---

[91] I did try Controlled folder access some time ago, and discovered that it interfered with some of the tools I use.

How Do I Decrypt Files Encrypted by Ransomware?

> **"**
> *... some of my files are gone, saying they have been encrypted with a public key. Files like my photos and so on. Of course they have a high fee in order for me to get them back. Do you have a solution?*

The news is not good, because no, I don't have a solution; there's just no good way to decrypt files encrypted by ransomware.

Prevention before the fact is the only guaranteed peace of mind on this one.

Encrypted by ransomware

Ransomware is a specific type of malware. It encrypts your files so you're unable to access or use them, and then offers to decrypt them if you pay the ransom.

Unfortunately, the technology used — "public key encryption" — is generally good. It's the same encryption technology you and I use to keep our data secure and our internet conversations private.

When done right, a file encrypted using public-key cryptography is essentially unrecoverable, unless you have the matching private key.

And needless to say, the hackers do it right. It's essentially impossible to decrypt files encrypted by ransomware without their private key.

Ransomware private key collections

As the threat and impact of ransomware has grown, security pros and authorities have been working to track down the hackers and take down their operations. On occasion, they succeed, and that specific ransomware threat is stopped.

When this happens, the private keys the hackers had are sometimes, though not always, discovered, and made available to the public.

The No More Ransom Project[92] maintains a database of known ransomware keys. Quoting their site:

"... it is *sometimes* possible to help infected users to regain access to their encrypted files or locked systems, without having to pay. We have created a repository of keys and applications that can decrypt data locked by different types of ransomware."

---

[92] https://go.askleo.com/nomoreransom

I've emphasized the word "sometimes" on purpose. There are no guarantees. In fact, in my experience, "sometimes" should really be "on rare occasions."

If your files are encrypted by ransomware, that's a straw worth grasping. In fact, if you haven't prepared ahead of time, it's really your only option.

Cures for ransomware

The best possible cure is to avoid having your files encrypted by ransomware in the first place. That means using the internet safely[93] and all that entails. Avoid malware, phishing schemes, and all the other ways that hackers get ransomware on to your machine.

The second best cure is to have a backup. If you find your computer afflicted with ransomware and your files encrypted, restoring them from a backup is the only 100% reliable recovery method.

And since ransomware can, in some (fortunately infrequent) cases, even encrypt your backups,[94] you need to understand and plan for a robust solution that allows you to recover. Normally this means automated daily backups and periodically making an offline copy, out of ransomware's reach.

Recovering from ransomware

By far, the simplest, fastest, most reliable solution to recovering files encrypted by ransomware is to restore them from a backup taken before the ransomware took hold. You restore the backup image of your entire machine to its state prior to the infection, and it's as if the ransomware never happened.

Hopefully, once restored, you'll know not to do whatever caused the infection in the first place.

If you don't have a complete image backup of your machine, but you do have a backup of your data, recovery is possible, albeit somewhat more work. I recommend that you:

- Take an image backup of the infected machine. This is to preserve a copy of the machine in its current state, in case it becomes necessary and possible to recover something from it in the future.
- Wipe the machine and install Windows from scratch.
- Install your applications from scratch.
- Restore your data.

If you have no backup of your data, things are significantly more dire.

---

[93] https://askleo.com/2374
[94] https://askleo.com/21259

Decrypting ransomware-encrypted files

As I said, there's no magical solution for decrypting a strongly encrypted file.[95] If you don't find the decryption key in a service like No More Ransom, then you're severely out of luck.

Which leaves the ultimate question: should you pay?

First, let's be clear: these are criminals you're thinking of dealing with. There's no guarantee that they'll follow through, should you elect to make payment. It could be the equivalent of simply throwing your money away.

Or ... it could recover your files.

Only you can decide whether or not to pay criminals the ransom.

My position is: don't do it. Doing so only encourages their criminal enterprise, and puts even more people at risk of finding their files encrypted by ransomware.

Instead, learn from the experience. Most importantly, *start backing up* so this never has to happen to you again.

---

[95] Of course, you may believe that the NSA or other government agencies might feel otherwise. I don't, but it doesn't matter: they're not going to help you here anyway.

Will Ransomware Encrypt my Backups?

> " *I wonder if a backup system that uses an external disk is safe from ransomware. I have Acronis True Image 2015 – paid version, and do a full backup once a month and an incremental daily. Can ransomware get to that backup? It is, in reality, just another disk in my system?*

The best we can say is ... maybe.

And even "maybe" has been slowly changing over time to something closer to "possibly".

It depends on a lot of different things, including the type of backup, where it's stored, and most importantly, the specific ransomware involved. There are many different types of ransomware, each with different characteristics.

Fortunately, there's a simple approach to keeping your backups safe.

Ransomware

Ransomware is malware that, once it infects your machine, begins encrypting files it finds there. Once done, it displays a message indicating your files have been encrypted. Your files are inaccessible to you until you pay a fee -- the ransom -- to get the decryption key.

One problem is that most ransomware is pretty good when it comes to encryption. There's little chance of somehow cracking the encryption to get your files back. Typically, you're left with three options:
- **Pay** the ransom. Strongly discouraged, as it encourages more attacks.
- **Restore** the files from a backup: strongly encouraged. This can make it all a non-issue, but requires that you have backups.
- **Give up**. Remove the malware, but live with the loss of whatever files were encrypted.

Relying on the backups, of course, assumes the backups themselves haven't been encrypted by the malware.

What ransomware encrypts

What we call "ransomware" is not a single thing. It's an entire class of malware that shares a particularly destructive behavior. There are hundreds, if not thousands, of different types of ransomware.

There are two very important ways they often differ: where they look for your files, and which files they choose to encrypt. What we call "ransomware" is not a single thing. In reality, ransomware is a class of malware, like any other, that happens to have particularly destructive behavior. There are hundreds, if not thousands, of different variations on ransomware.

Two of those variations are central to this discussion: which drives they encrypt, and which files they encrypt.

Drives scanned

Most current variations of ransomware scan only your system drive. For most systems, that's the "C:" drive. Any other drives -- including your backup drive -- are ignored. This allows the ransomware to be fast, encrypting before you notice, while still giving it access to your important files, typically also stored on C:.

More sophisticated variations that can scan all drives attached to the system, including external and/or network connections, do exist. Anything with a drive letter could be at risk.

One small bit of good news is only drives are scanned. Storage accessed only via your browser or a dedicated application, such as some forms of cloud storage and online backup services, are not directly at risk. There's still bad news, however, since if those services mirror or back up files on one of your drives, it's very likely they'll mirror or back up the files once they've been encrypted, perhaps overwriting previously saved, unencrypted backups.

Files encrypted

Ransomware does not encrypt all files.

This fact is often overlooked when folks are busy panicking over ransomware in general. But of course ransomware can't encrypt everything; Windows itself needs to keep working, as does whatever mechanism the ransomware uses to display its demands and recover your files if you pay up.

In general, ransomware targets what I call "potentially high value" files, based on the filename extension:

- Documents such as ".doc", ".docx", ".txt", and more.
- Spreadsheets and finance databases like ".xls", ".xlsx", ".qbw", and more (particularly impactful for businesses).
- Photos, including ".jpg", ".jpeg", and more (particularly impactful for individuals with precious family photos).

This isn't meant to be an exhaustive list, by any stretch, but it points out that not all files are always at risk.

In fact, if you're using an image backup program, it's worth noticing that I didn't list ".tib" (Acronis's format), ".mrimg" (Macrium Reflect) or ".pbd" (EaseUS Todo). More often than not, these files are *not* encrypted. Why? Well, since they're typically large, the encryption process could take quite a bit of time, making it more likely to be detected before it does its damage.

So there are three possibilities for those backup image files:

So there are three possibilities for those backup image files:
- They'll be ignored. This is still the most common.
- They'll be encrypted. This can happen, but is less frequent.
- They'll be deleted. This is rarer still, but still lands you without a backup.

While it's infrequent, ransomware can encrypt backups, but we don't know if it will. The best we can say is "maybe".

What it takes for backups to be encrypted

In order to truly put your backups at risk:
1. The ransomware variant needs to scan more drives that just the C: drive.
2. The ransomware variant needs to specifically choose to encrypt backup image files.

Most ransomware today does not have both those characteristics.

But *most* is not *all*. You could encounter ransomware that encrypts your backups; it's just not likely currently.

How to protect yourself

The knee-jerk reaction to hearing that backups *might* get encrypted is to disconnect the backup drive when you're not actually making a backup.

Don't do that.[96]

The problem with that is the backups are no longer automated. You have to *remember* to re-attach the drive in order to back up. Forgive me, but I don't want to rely on your memory—or mine, for that matter—to perform backups. Especially when, today at least, the risk we're trying to avoid is relatively small.

My recommendation:
- Keep backing up as you do: automated, with your backup drive continually attached.
- Every so often, make a copy of your backups "somewhere else": to some source which is then disconnected. It could be another drive, another machine on your network, whatever. One approach is to have two backup drives, but only connect one at a time, and swap them every week or two.

Don't get me wrong: the risk of ransomware encrypting your backup exists, but it's on the low end of the scale. It's much more important that your automated backups continue to help you recover from more likely issues.

Of course, the best defense is to never get ransomware (or any malware) in the first place, and stay safe in general.

---

[96] https://askleo.com/18248

Protecting with Updates

How Do I Make Sure Windows is Up to Date?

> " *How do I make sure Windows is up-to-date? And ... should I?*

The last question is easy to answer: yes. Yes, you absolutely should keep Windows as up-to-date as possible.

I know there are those who disagree. Some go so far as to seek out ways to prevent Windows 10 from updating itself.

Let's look at why they feel that way, and what I believe you should do.

Vulnerabilities and updates

The issue is common to all software: no one is perfect. All software has bugs, period, no exceptions.[97]

While many bugs are minor and inconsequential, some make the software vulnerable to exploitation by people trying to do something bad, like hack into your system, steal your data, use your computer to send spam, or worse. These bugs are often referred to as "vulnerabilities", and the software that takes advantage of them is termed "malicious software", or simply "malware".

When vulnerabilities are found, manufacturers release updates to their software that fix (or "patch") the bug.

It's important that users of affected software install those updates when they're made available.

Unfortunately, some individuals do not install updates, for a variety of reasons. This leaves their computers vulnerable to more and more malware, even though the associated bugs the malware can exploit have been fixed.

Automating updates

Windows Update is Microsoft's solution to update distribution and installation.

---

[97] If someone claims that a particular bit of software has no bugs, then either they simply haven't yet found the bugs that actually are there anyway, or they've dismissed some erroneous or unexpected behavior (aka a bug) as not rising to the level of being called a bug. It's still a bug.

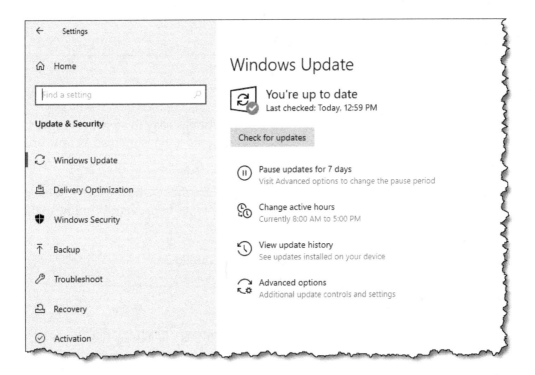

It runs in the background, periodically checking for updates to Windows[98] that apply to your machine's particular configuration. When available updates are found, Windows Update downloads and installs them automatically.

It's not uncommon for updates to require your machine to be rebooted. Software cannot be updated if it's in use. That means in order to update core components of Windows itself, Windows needs to shut down briefly. That's a reboot..

Updates and failures

I said earlier that all software has bugs.

Updates are no exception. They are software, so they could have bugs. The update process itself could have bugs.

The net result is from time to time, or perhaps from person to person, Windows Updates are sometimes considered "risky". There's a perception that with any update, there's a risk your machine could become less stable. In the worst cases, Windows updates have completely crashed the machine on which they've been installed.

That bad reputation — warranted or not — has had serious, long-term consequences.

---

[98] And, optionally, other Microsoft software.

Failures to update

Because of that bad reputation, some computer users would delay their updates to what they considered to be a safe time—after some period of time had passed that allowed them to feel confident that the update would not harm their machine.

Others stopped taking updates altogether.

Needless to say, the authors of malware approve. To them, delaying or skipping updates means that once a vulnerability is discovered, they can continue to write and circulate malware to exploit it, because they know not everyone will take the update that fixes it.

Applying updates regularly remains the best approach to keeping your system secure and up-to-date. I continue to recommend that you let Windows update itself automatically, so you don't have to take any action at all. As we'll see in a moment, Microsoft agrees—strongly.

Perhaps a bit too strongly.

Perception and reality

Windows 10 is installed on close to, if not over, a billion machines world-wide. That means when there's even a hint of a problem, it makes headlines everywhere. The size or scope of the problem is immaterial to the headline writers — every failure is treated as a big deal, if not a disaster.

To be fair, even if one tenth of one percent of all Windows 10 machines suffered a failure due to Windows Update, that's still a million machines. That's a lot.

And yet, everything else being equal,[99] you run only a 1 in 1,000 chance of having a problem.

Still, because of headlines and reputation, some users delay updates to what they consider a safer time — a few days or weeks later. In some cases, they try not to take updates at all.

Malware authors approve. To them, delaying or skipping updates means once a vulnerability is discovered, they can continue to write and circulate malware to exploit it, because they know not everyone will take the update to fix it. If you pay attention to notifications of large data breaches in the news and dig deep enough, you'll often find that hackers gained access via a vulnerability for which a patch had been made available, but had not yet been applied.

Applying updates regularly remains the best approach to keeping your system secure and up to date. I continue to recommend you let Windows update itself automatically, so you don't have to take any action at all.

---

[99] With no specific characteristics to refine the number, it's 1 in 1,000. However, it often becomes quickly apparent that a failure applies to certain machines, or certain characteristics of machines, meaning you can much more accurately judge the risk you actually face. Typically, you have even less risk than 1 in 1,000.

Windows 10 and forced automated updates

Windows 10 originally had no option to delay updates in its consumer ("Home") editions. Updates were downloaded and installed automatically.

In a perfect world, this would be a perfect solution. Unfortunately, we do not live in a perfect world.

There have been two major issues:

- While the stability of Windows updates have improved over time — fewer and fewer updates cause significant problems — some Windows 10 updates, at least initially, seemed a step backwards. Reports of people having problems after an update seemed to increase.
- Updates requiring a reboot would indeed reboot, often at an inconvenient time.

The stability of updates appears to be improving once again, and Microsoft has made additional options available.

In Settings, Windows Update, you'll find an option to "Pause updates for 7 days".

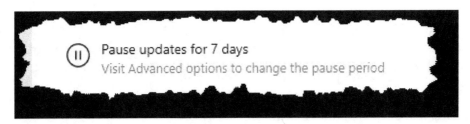

This is particularly useful if your computer usage is about to be particularly sensitive or important; you know you won't be impacted by an update.

Similarly, Microsoft added the concept of "active hours".

But the bottom line is that Microsoft really, really, REALLY wants you to keep your machine as up-to-date as possible.

This allows you to tell Windows Update when you normally use your computer. It will not reboot the computer during this time.

In **Advanced Options**, you'll find the following options.

- "Show a notification when your PC requires a restart to finish updating". This allows you to control when your machine will reboot, allowing you to save your work and make sure nothing will be negatively impacted by the reboot.

- An option to "Pause updates". This is the same as the setting above, but allows you to pause updates for up to 35 days if need be.

The bottom line is that Microsoft really, really, REALLY wants you to keep your machine as up to date as possible. And I agree.

Recommendation: managing risk

It's all about risk management: trading off the risk of a misbehaving update to the risk of having an unpatched vulnerability exploited by malware.

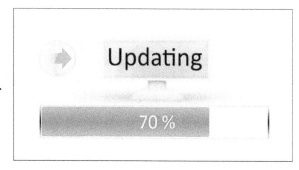

The good news is, we know how to manage risk.

For all versions of Windows, my recommendation remains:

1. Back up regularly. Ideally, perform system image backups[100] as I've outlined in several articles. Then, no matter what, you're protected from any kind of failure, be it hardware failure, a crashed disk, malware, or even a troublesome Windows update.
2. Configure Windows to notify you when a restart is required, and restart as soon as is practical. This places the restart and its impact completely under your control.
3. Don't delay updates if you don't have to, and if you do, choose the smallest length of time you can. This minimizes the length of time you leave your machine exposed to known vulnerabilities.
4. Don't try to disable Windows Update. It's critical to your safety.

In my opinion, this is the safest approach to managing a wide variety of risks related to using your computer—not just the risks of a failed update.

---

[100] https://askleo.com/4473

I Got Burned by Windows Update. Should I Just Avoid It?

> " *I recently took an update via Windows Update, and after doing so, my machine wouldn't even boot. It took a technician hours to get it working again. That's not something I can afford to have happen again. I'm avoiding Windows Update from here on out.*

That's a conglomeration of a variety of questions and problem reports I've received over the years. The pace picked up when Windows 10 was released.

Windows Update has a reputation for occasionally causing working systems to fail. The good news is, it's almost always a tiny percentage of machines affected. The bad news is, that's no solace if you're affected.

I absolutely sympathize. I can understand why you'd be skittish about ever taking an update again.

And yet, you should.

What happened?

Unfortunately, as unlikely as they might be, there are many reasons Windows Update might fail. Malware, for example.

Contrary to the opinion of those who've been burned, each update is tested before it's released. Microsoft used to do extensive testing itself, and now relies on members of the "Insider Program" for that testing.

Even with many people participating, it's still impossible to cover every possible configuration. Most of Windows 10's update issues in recent years have been related to specific combinations of hardware.

It's impossible to test for everything, and just as impossible to predict whether something bad will happen to you.

By and large, Windows Update is reliable and robust. However, if you're in the minority of people who have experienced an issue, you probably don't feel that way.

Avoiding Windows Update

I'm certainly not saying that it's foolish to avoid Windows Update once you've had a bad experience. It's a natural reaction to what can be a very serious and time-consuming situation

But I will definitely say that avoiding updates long term is ill-advised.

The problem is that keeping your system up to date is *critical* to keeping it safe from malware. You want the security updates that are regularly and routinely made available via Windows Update.

You simply *must* keep your system up to date.

Cleaning up and continuing to use Windows Update

If Windows Update causes problems on your machine, the easiest way to recover is to restore to a full-system backup taken prior to the update.

If that sounds familiar, it's because it's the same advice for removing malware: restore to a backup taken prior to the malware's arrival.

The irony is not lost on me.[101]

> Working on updates
> 30% complete
> Don't turn off your computer

If you don't have a full-system backup image, things are significantly more difficult.

In the worst case, you may need to back up your data, reinstall Windows[102] from scratch, and then get current with updates before continuing. This may also clear up whatever problem might have caused the update to fail in the first place.

If that's not in the cards, you may be faced with researching the specific failure and seeing if others have ways to resolve or work around the problem.

If the problem is due to an error on Microsoft's part, you might want to delay updates[103] by a week or two after you recover. Updates causing widespread failures are themselves quickly updated and fixed.

Moving forward

Begin backing up[104] regularly. Start today. Daily system image backups are best, so that you can restore your machine to a pre-problem state, regardless of whether that problem is a bad update, malware, or something else entirely.

Keep Windows Updates turned on -- meaning, don't try and apply the various hacks that claim to turn it off completely and permanently. If your version of Windows supports it, you can delay updates for some amount of time without turning it off completely. Once the delay has passed, back up and take the updates offered.

I do believe that Microsoft needs to do a better job[105] of making Windows Update more robust and trustworthy. This is especially true now, since much of its operation in Windows 10 is not optional. It doesn't take many failures for its reputation to be further tarnished. The result is that users take ill-advised measures and end up putting themselves at even greater risk in other ways.

---

[101] That a Windows Update might be considered "malware" by some.
[102] https://askleo.com/23277
[103] If your version of Windows allows you that level of control.
[104] https://askleo.com/30103
[105] https://askleo.com/65097

Where Do I Get Driver Updates? Where to Find Them AND Places to Avoid

> **"** *I downloaded 3 separate 'check drivers' programs. Each program identified seven drivers as being outdated. However, my Device Manager says they're OK. It's been very difficult to find the drivers, and if they are outdated I will have to purchase one of the driver programs. Do I need to update these drivers? If so, how do I find the sites to download?*

Device Manager will not tell you whether or not a device driver is out of date; that's not its job. What it tells you is if the device driver is installed and working at some basic level.

Finding out whether your device drivers are out of date isn't that simple, and neither is getting the updates.

I'll review the options and describe what I do.

Driver?

A quickie refresher: Windows is designed to work with all sorts of hardware—even hardware that might not exist yet.

Windows manages to do this by writing programs to use a fairly generic, albeit complex, interface. When you set up the machine or install new hardware, software translates those generic instructions into whatever the actual hardware on the machine requires.

That low-level software that directly controls your hardware device is called a device driver, or just "driver" for short.[106]

For example, your video card has software that knows how to translate generic Windows instructions to "draw a pixel here", or "change the resolution to this" into the specific instructions required by the specific video card in your computer. Different video card, different driver, but Windows and Windows programs still do the same things the same generic way.

Some key points:
- Drivers are software.
- Drivers are specific to the hardware for which they're designed.
- Drivers, like any software, can have bugs and security vulnerabilities. That means every so often they need updates.

That means every so often, they need updates.

---

[106] You may also hear the terms "hardware driver" or even "software driver".

Is A Driver Out of Date?

The real question is, "How do I know if there's a more up-to-date version of the device drivers that are installed on my machine?"

If the drivers were installed with Windows itself, your answer is very simple: Windows Update will handle any updates for you. That's all most people need to do.

If your drivers were not installed as part of Windows — and it can be hard to tell — things get more complicated.

There are several third-party tools that may tell you, and I *never, ever* use them.

I find most to be the classic "We'll tell you what's wrong for free, but if you want us to fix it, it'll cost you money" model. There's not really anything inherently wrong with that approach, but it certainly rubs me the wrong way. Some are scams, or close to it.

So I avoid the entire class of scanning tools falling into that model. I recommend you avoid them as well.

When it comes to drivers, not knowing if a driver is out of date doesn't really bother me much.

If It ain't broke, don't fix it. but if it's broke...

I look for driver updates *only* when I'm trying to track down a problem with a specific driver or device.

In other words, if things are working, I leave well enough alone.

I realize that's at odds with the "keep your system updated for safety" mantra which I and others seem to harp on. My thinking is simply this:

- The majority of drivers are already handled by Windows Update. While newer drivers are often available directly from hardware manufacturers, issues dealing with security—the only thing I care about, if I'm not having other problems—are more than likely pushed through the Windows Update pipeline.
- Drivers not handled by Windows Update are diverse enough that targeting any one of them for a potential security vulnerability just isn't worth most hackers' time. Effort spent creating malware for a specific video driver, for example, targets only those people with that driver, and then only if that driver is not updated by Windows Update.
- Historically, driver updates are risky. Driver updates that come directly from manufacturers often don't have the wide breadth of testing that ensures they'll work properly on my machine. Put another way: updating drivers without reason can be risky.

Where to find drivers

As you might guess, I don't recommend paying driver download utilities to do the work for you. Some may be legitimate and work, but in my opinion, it's too risky for a couple of reasons:

- They may not be legitimate or work.
- You don't know where they get their drivers, or indeed, if the drivers they provide are even up to date.

If you're going to go somewhere other than Windows Update for drivers, I can only recommend one destination: the hardware manufacturer.

Start with the computer manufacturer, especially if yours is a name brand computer. They often provide all the drivers on their support site. Others will point you to the component manufacturer's site—perhaps even directly to the page you need.

And yes, if the computer manufacturer doesn't help with either direct downloads or point to the right component manufacturer, then this gets old very fast... which is another reason I only recommend doing it if you're actually chasing down a problem you're having with a specific piece of hardware.

If that's not the case, then the best place to get driver updates is simple: nowhere at all.

Part 4: Protect Your Laptop

How Do I Use an Open Wi-Fi Hotspot Safely?

> " *I've returned to the same coffee shop where I was a few months ago when I noticed that my email had been hijacked/hacked. This time, I'm using my phone, but the last time, when I noticed the hack, I was using my computer and doing email over an open-internet, free Wi-Fi network.*
>
> *Do you think that could be the source of the problem or just a coincidence? I'm still afraid to do email from here.*

It definitely could have been.

Unfortunately, it's hard to say for sure, and it could have been something else unrelated.

As we can't really diagnose the past, let's look ahead instead.

It can be absolutely safe to send and receive email, or even other tasks, from a coffee shop or other location that provides unsecured or "open" Wi-Fi. In fact, I do it all the time.

But you do have to follow some *very* important practices to ensure your safety.

The open Wi-Fi problem

The problem with open Wi-Fi hotspots is that the wireless radio connection between your computer and the wireless access point nearby is not encrypted. That means any data you don't actively encrypt some other way is transmitted in the clear, and *anyone within range can eavesdrop* and see it. Encryption prevents that.

Important: know if it is encrypted or not. If you **connect** to a hotspot and *the operating system on your machine* requires a password for it to work, that's not an open Wi-Fi hotspot, and you may be OK. On the other hand, if you can connect without a password, and your browser immediately takes you to a *webpage* that says, "enter a password" (as in a hotel) or "check to accept our terms" (as in most other open hotspots) **it** is not encrypted **and it is not secure**. It is an *open* Wi-Fi hotspot.

Turn on the firewall

Fortunately, firewalls are "on" by default in most operating systems.

However, when you're at home, you may use your router as your firewall, and keep any software firewall on your machine disabled. That works well, as the router stops network-based attacks before they ever reach your computer—while you're at home.

When you're on an open Wi-Fi hotspot, or connected directly to the internet via other means, that software firewall is *critical*.

Make *sure* your firewall is enabled before connecting to an open Wi-Fi hotspot. Various network-based threats could be present on an untrusted connection, and it's the firewall's job to protect you from that.

Secure your desktop email program

If you use a desktop email program, such as Outlook, Windows Live Mail, Thunderbird, or others, you *must* make certain it is configured to use SSL/secure connections for sending and downloading email.

Typically, that means that when you configure each email account in your email program, you need to:

- Configure your POP3 or IMAP server for accessing your email using the SSL, TLS, or SSL/TLS security options, and usually a different port number.
- Configure your SMTP server for sending email using SSL, TLS, or SSL/TLS security options, and usually a different port number, such as 26, 465, or 587, instead of the default 25.

How you configure these settings depends on the email program you use. The specific settings depend on the email service.

Once configured with the proper settings, you can feel secure downloading and sending mail using an open Wi-Fi hotspot.

Secure your web-based email

If you use a web-based email service like Gmail, Outlook.com, Yahoo, or others via your browser, you *must* make sure it uses an httpS connection. Fortunately, most all major email services now rely on https.

In years past, accessing email using a plain http connection might well have been the source of many open Wi-Fi-related hacks: usernames and passwords are visible to any hackers in range who cared to look. Https prevents that.

Secure all your other online accounts

Any and all web-based (aka "cloud") services that require you to log in with a username and password should either be used only with https from start to finish, or be avoided completely while you're using an open Wi-Fi hotspot.

With more and more services provided online, this is getting to be a larger problem. Fortunately, most are aware of the issue and are using https properly.

Using the cloud is a great way to manage your digital life from wherever you may be, but security remains key. Using https is critical when you're out and about.

Use a VPN

This one's for the road warriors. You know them: the folks who are always traveling and online the entire time, often hopping from coffee shop to coffee shop in search of an internet connection as they go.

A VPN, or Virtual Private Network, is a service that sets up a securely encrypted 'tunnel' to the internet and routes *all* of your internet traffic through it. Https or not, SSL/secure email configuration or not, all of your traffic is securely tunneled, and no one sharing that open Wi-Fi hotspot can see a thing.

This service typically involves a recurring fee.[107] As I said, they're great for road warriors, but probably overkill for the rest of us, as long as we follow the other security steps described above.

A VPN also has the side effect of protecting you not only from the hacker in the corner, but from the coffee shop IT guy or whoever is providing the internet connection.

Use different passwords

Finally, it's important to keep your account passwords different from each other[108] and, of course, secure.[109]

That way, should one account be compromised by some stroke of misfortune, the hackers won't automatically gain access to your other accounts.

Remember, even when you use an open Wi-Fi hotspot properly, a hacker can still see the sites you're visiting, even though they cannot see what you are sending to and from that site. That means they'll know exactly what sites to target next.

Consider not using free Wi-Fi at all

As I said, it can be safe to use open Wi-Fi, but it's also very easy for it to be unsafe.

One very common and solid one solution is to use your phone instead.

While it is technically possible, a mobile/cellular network connection is *significantly* less likely to be hacked. In fact, I use this solution heavily when I travel.

---

[107] In fact, I'd avoid free VPNs, as they run a higher risk of tracking or exposing your information in other ways.
[108] https://askleo.com/11788
[109] https://askleo.com/4844

Most mobile carriers offer one or more of the following options:

- Use your mobile device. Many phones or other mobile devices, such as iPhones, iPads, Android-based phones, and others are quite capable email and web-surfing devices, and typically do so via the mobile network. (Some also use Wi-Fi, so be certain you're using the mobile broadband connection to avoid the very security issues we're discussing.)
- Tether your phone. Tethering means you connect your phone to your computer—usually by a USB cable, but in some cases, via a Bluetooth connection—and the phone acts as a modem, providing a mobile broadband internet connection.
- Use a dedicated mobile modem. These are USB devices that attach to your computer and act as a modem to provide a mobile broadband internet connection, much like tethering your phone.
- Use a mobile hotspot. In lieu of tethering, many phones now have the ability to act as a Wi-Fi hotspot themselves. There are also dedicated devices, such as the MiFi, that are simple dedicated hotspots. Either way, the device connects to the mobile broadband network and provides a Wi-Fi hotspot accessible to one or more devices within range. When used in this manner, these devices are acting as routers and must be configured securely,[110] including a WPA2 password, so as not to be another *open* Wi-Fi hotspot susceptible to hacking.

I travel with a MiFi, and also have a phone capable of acting as a hotspot as a backup. I find this to be the most flexible option for the way I travel and use my computer.

Don't forget physical security

Laptops are convenient because they're portable. And because they're portable, they're also easily stolen.

Unfortunately, it only takes a few seconds for an unattended laptop to disappear. I never leave mine alone: even if I need to make a quick trip to the restroom, the laptop comes with me. There's just no way of knowing that absolutely everyone around me is trustworthy.

In that same vein, I also prepare in case my laptop does get swiped. Specifically, that means:
- My hard drive is encrypted.
- My sensitive data is stored in folders that are encrypted using BoxCryptor. Those folders are not mounted unless I need something.
- LastPass, my password management software, is set to require a password re-prompt after a certain amount of inactivity.
- I have two-factor authentication enabled on as many accounts as support it, including LastPass.
- I have tracking/remote wiping software installed.

Computer theft and recovery is a larger topic that's only tangential to using open Wi-Fi hotspots. Clearly, though, if you are a frequent user of assorted open hotspots in your community or when you travel, a little attention to theft prevention and recovery is worthwhile.

---

[110] https://askleo.com/11107

Security and convenience are always at odds

As you can see, it's easy to get this stuff wrong, since doing it securely takes a little planning and forethought.

But it's important. If you're not doing things securely, that guy in the corner with his laptop open could be watching all your internet traffic on the Wi-Fi connection, *including your account username and password* as they fly by.

And when that happens, you can get hacked.

Fortunately, with a little knowledge and preparation, it's relatively easy to be safe.

Can Hotel Internet Traffic Be Sniffed?

> **"**
> *My friend's husband has been getting into her email even though she's not given him her password. He has confronted his sister about an email and when asked how he got into the email he says that where he works (a large hotel chain), they have a program that searches emails for keywords and brings info up. Could that be true? Can they snoop on hotel internet traffic?*

Yes.

Hotel internet security is one of the most overlooked risks travelers face. I'm not just talking wireless— I'm talking *any* internet connection provided by your hotel.

In fact, I'm actually writing this in a hotel room, and yes, I have taken a few precautions.

It's as bad as open Wi-Fi

I'll put it bluntly: *hotel internet connections are just as unsafe as an unsecured "open" wireless hotspot.*

Any hotel internet connection, wired or not.

There are two basic issues.

1: Your ISP can see everything you do. [111]

When you're in a hotel, that hotel is your ISP. They provide the connectivity, routers, and other equipment that connect you to the internet.

Thus, like your traditional ISP, they have the ability to monitor any and all traffic on the network.

You need to realize it's *their* network you're using. They own it, control it, and they have the right to monitor its usage.

Unfortunately, it also means employees can abuse their power to go snooping.

2: Your neighbors may also be able to see everything you do.

This is less common. Depending on exactly how the hotel network is configured, it's possible that you and the rooms around you are connected through a hub. The "problem" with a hub is that it's a dumb device;[112] it sends everything it gets to everything connected to it.

---

[111] https://askleo.com/3004
[112] https://askleo.com/1862

When you send data through the hub, not only does the upstream internet connection see the data, as you want, but that data is also sent down the wires to neighboring rooms. Computer there *should* ignore it, but it's there for the taking. This is *exactly* like connecting via an open WiFi connection, where anyone in range can "sniff" your internet traffic.

Staying safe while at a hotel

So, what do you do?

Follow all the steps one should take to stay safe using an open Wi-Fi hotspot.[113]

Use a firewall. Make sure your Windows or other software firewall is enabled. The good news is that this is typically on by default.

Use https. Only access sensitive websites using an http**s** connection. This includes both sensitive sites like banking, as well as common things like email. The good news is that this is typically the default for most websites these days.

Encrypt your email connection. If you're using a desktop email program downloading email via POP3 or IMAP, or sending email via SMTP, make sure those connections are encrypted. Check with your email provider for the appropriate settings. The good news is that most email services provide them.

Consider a VPN. A Virtual Private Network encrypts all of your communications through the hotel's network. The bad news is that this is an additional service you sign up for.

Consider not using the hotel's network. If your smartphone can be used as a Wi-Fi hotspot, or if you can perform all of your tasks on your mobile device using your data plan, you'll bypass the hotel completely.

What I do

When I run an actual email program, such as Thunderbird, I make sure to configure mail server connections to use an SSL encrypted connection. My mail is secure.

For encrypted websites (those using https) I do nothing, other than make sure the connection remains "https" as I navigate from page to page.

For unencrypted (http without the s) websites, I do one of three things:
- Avoid anything that might be considered secure or sensitive.
- Use a VPN.
- Use my mobile connection instead.

---

[113] https://askleo.com/4790

It's more than just hotels

I've been talking about security in the context of hotels, since it's common for the traveling public to rely on the internet provided by the facility in which they're staying.

All of this applies to *any* internet connection provided by anyone. Everywhere, from a coffee shop or airport Wi-Fi to the internet provided by convention centers, libraries, and other public facilities, there's an IT department in the background able to examine your unencrypted internet traffic.

Whether or not they would take the time to do so is unknown, but as our original questioner found out, sometimes they do.

It pays to be aware and make conscious, hopefully secure decisions regarding your security wherever you connect.

How Can I Keep Data on My Laptop Secure?

> " *I travel a lot, and have sensitive data on the laptop I take with me that I need as part of my job. But I'm in fear of losing the laptop and that this data will fall into the wrong hands. What do you suggest?*

I know how you feel. I also have sensitive information on my laptop that I would prefer not to fall into the wrong hands. I can handle losing the laptop, but thinking about the data in the wrong hands ... well ... that would be bad.

I've used different solutions over the years, and they all share one thing in common: encryption.

Encrypting individual files

You could, of course, encrypt data using various archiving tools that allow you to assign the resulting file a password.

The most common approach is to use "zip" files, with tools like 7-Zip.[114] The zip file format supports password protection, which encrypts the file's contents. Originally, zip encryption was weak and easily cracked, but over the years it's improved to be pretty good.

The problem with individual file encryption is you must manually decrypt the file to use it. This also means you need to re-encrypt it when you're done, and erase all traces of the work you did — such as temporary files — that might be left unencrypted.

Individual file encryption is appropriate for some things, but for frequent use, it's typically too cumbersome.

Encryption of individual files offered by specific applications — such as password protection in Microsoft Office documents — can be good. Unfortunately, it can also be bad. Older versions of Office, for example, were quite poor at encryption. Current versions are better. If you go this route, you're at the mercy of the individual application vendors' expertise. I prefer dedicated encryption tools.

Encrypting the entire hard disk

Encrypting the entire hard drive using whole-drive encryption is the other extreme. It is one way to protect the contents of your *entire* system.

System-provided solutions, like Bitlocker in Windows, use encryption keys based on your system login to encrypt the hard drive. If you can't log in, you can't access your data; it's simple as that. It also protects your data should your hard disk be removed and attached to another computer.

---

[114] https://askleo.com/2856

If you lose your log-in account for any reason, you can lose access to your data permanently. BitLocker encourages you to back up the encryption key separately when you first encrypt your drive. If you use BitLocker, I strongly recommend you do so.

Third-party tools like VeraCrypt also support whole-drive encryption. This is independent of your system login and uses a secure passphrase to decrypt the drive and boot your system.

Important: your data is fully secure only if you *log out or shut down*. As long as you are logged in and able to access your data yourself, it's available in unencrypted form. Avoid states like Sleep or Hibernate, neither of which is an actual logout.

Whole-disk encryption is what I now use on my laptop, making sure to log out and shut down completely when appropriate.

Encrypted vaults

For many years I used TrueCrypt. While TrueCrypt itself is no longer supported,[115] derivatives like VeraCrypt are, and are quite worthy successors.

VeraCrypt is free, open source, on-the-fly encryption software. It provides serious, industrial-strength encryption, while still being fairly easy to use.

The two most common ways it is used are:
- To encrypt an entire disk volume, such as a USB thumb drive, single partition, or entire hard disk, as I described above.
- To create an encrypted virtual disk "volume" or container.

It's the latter approach I use, as it makes it easy to copy entire containers from machine to machine.

An encrypted virtual disk is simply a file that VeraCrypt "mounts" as an additional drive letter on your machine. You specify the passphrase when the virtual drive is mounted, and the unencrypted contents of the container appear as another drive on your system.

For example, you might create an encrypted drive in a file: c:\windowssecritstuf. If someone were to look at the contents of that file directly, they would see only random gibberish—the result of encryption. When mounted by VeraCrypt, it appears as a virtual drive—for example, selecting the drive letter "P:". Drive P: would look and operate like any other disk, and would contain the unencrypted contents of the encrypted drive. Encryption is as simple as moving or copying a file to the drive.

---

[115] https://askleo.com/14720

The trick for security is to never mount the drive automatically. When your machine boots up, "P:", for example, would be nowhere to be found. The file c:\windowssecritstuf would be present, but only visible as encrypted gibberish. If someone stole your machine, that's all they would find.

Only after you've used VeraCrypt to select the file (c:\windowssecritstuf), chosen to mount it as (P:), and supplied the correct passphrase would the virtual drive be mounted and the encrypted data accessible.

Encryption for the cloud

Yet another solution to laptop security leverages a tool meant to keep your data secure in the cloud: BoxCryptor.

You can think of BoxCryptor as a kind of hybrid combination of VeraCrypt's vault with individual file encryption. (BoxCryptor: Secure Your Data in the Cloud[116] has a more detailed comparison.)

Instead of a file, you point BoxCryptor at a folder — generally a folder in one of the online cloud storage services, like OneDrive — and it mounts that folder as a virtual drive. The data in the actual OneDrive folder is encrypted, and the virtual drive gives transparent access to the encrypted data, much like a VeraCrypt volume. Unlike VeraCrypt, the files are encrypted individually. When a file changes, only that file needs to be updated with the cloud provider.

While BoxCryptor is designed specifically to keep your cloud data secure, there's nothing that says you can't use it for other purposes. You can point it at any folder on your computer and have BoxCryptor manage encrypting the contents.

Particularly if you're already using BoxCryptor for your cloud data, you won't have to install any other software to encrypt local data

Encryption and security caveats

Most all of the approaches are relatively straightforward. The tradeoff is complexity in setup versus complexity to use.

But there are additional items to keep in mind whenever you secure your system in this way.
- Passphrases are the weakest link. Encryption does not make a bad passphrase any more secure. If you choose an obvious passphrase, a dictionary attack can certainly be used to unlock your encrypted volume or decrypt your encrypted file.
- Encrypted volumes and encrypted files do you no good if the files you care about are *also* elsewhere on your machine in some *un*encrypted form. This is one of the benefits of whole-disk encryption—it's *all* encrypted, no matter what.
- You *must* back up. Preferably keep the backups *un*encrypted but secure in some other way, in case you lose your computer, your encrypted disk or files, or if you forget your password. Without the password, encrypted data is *not* recoverable.

---

[116] https://askleo.com/5722

Data encryption is an important part of an overall security strategy. Keeping your sensitive data secure requires a little forethought and planning. With viruses and spyware running amok, not to mention theft, there's no excuse not to take a little time now to save yourself some serious grief later, should the unthinkable happen.

What Can a Computer Thief See If I Password Protect My Windows Sign-in?

> **"** *My mid-tower computer was recently stolen in a burglary. The Windows system was password-protected at start-up. What files can be accessed by those trying to enter the system?*

It'll take a computer-savvy thief less than five minutes to gain access to everything on your computer.

Yep. Everything.

Everything you haven't otherwise protected, that is.

Physical security

There's a fundamental concept that I remind people of from time to time. It's simply this:

If it's not physically secure, it's not secure.

I normally bring that up when people have questions relating to sharing a computer, or perhaps sharing living space, and being somewhat concerned about what a roommate might or might not have access to when they're not around. Most commonly, it applies to laptops and mobile devices.

The short version is that if someone has physical access to your computer, they can quickly gain access to *everything* on it.

Of course, computer theft is the very definition of physical access.

Gaining access

There are several ways that someone can gain access to your computer's contents:

- They can reboot from a CD or USB device and reset the administrative log-in password. In fact, it's so easy, here are the instructions: I've Lost the Password to My Windows Administrator Account, How Do I Get It Back?[117] The newer UEFI "Secure Boot" prevents this, if enabled.
- They can reboot from a Linux live CD and access the contents of your hard drive without needing to log in to Windows at all. Again, "Secure Boot", when enabled, is intended to prevent this.

---

[117] https://askleo.com/3379

- They can remove the hard disk from your machine, connect it to another, and once again access the contents of your hard disk without needing to log in to your copy of Windows at all.

All that should be pretty scary, mostly because it is.

If it's not physically secure, it's not secure.

Keeping your data secure

So what do you do?

Well, in an after-the-fact case like you're asking about, it's too late. The computer has already been stolen. What's important is that you know the data on it could be accessed by whoever has the machine now. If you have personal and confidential information on it, it's time to assume it's been completely compromised. It may not be. It may not be *yet*. It may never be. But you must assume the worst.

There are three approaches to keeping your data secure:
- Secure the machine.
- Encrypt the hard drive.
- Secure your data.

Secure the machine

Securing your machine means doing things like bolting it down, attaching it to something with a security cable, or putting it in a locked room or cabinet. (Make sure that the machine has enough ventilation if you put it in any enclosed space.)

These aren't perfect solutions, as a very determined thief might still circumvent these measures, but they'll at least stop the casual burglar by making it easier to steal something else.

Encrypt the hard drive

Encrypting the entire hard drive using whole-drive encryption is one way to protect the contents of your entire system.

With an encrypted hard drive, even moving the hard drive to a different machine doesn't help a thief, because all they would see is random, nonsensical data.

There are two approaches to whole-drive encryption: system-provided, and third party tools.

System solutions (like BitLocker for Windows[118]) use encryption keys based on your system login to encrypt the hard drive. If you can't log in, then you can't access your data. If you lose your log-in account *for any reason*, you can lose access to your data. You are encouraged to back up the encryption key separately, which would restore access.

---

[118] Or FileVault, on a Mac.

Third-party tools like VeraCrypt[119] also support whole-drive encryption. This is independent of your system login, and typically relies on selecting an appropriately secure passphrase to decrypt the drive and boot your system.

Important: In both cases, your data is fully secure *only if you log out*. As long as you are logged in and can access your data yourself, it's available in unencrypted form. You may want to avoid Sleep and Hibernate, neither of which is an actual logout.

Also important: BIOS or other pre-boot passwords may *or may not* be a form of protection. Some, but not all, include hard disk encryption. You'll have to check your system's documentation to determine that for your specific machine.

Encrypt your data

The good news about whole-drive encryption is that once enabled, it's relatively transparent. The bad news is that losing access to your data can be a tad easier, and depending on the technique, completely encrypted drives can be somewhat less resilient to hardware failures.[120]

The compromise is to encrypt only parts of what you keep on the machine: your data.

To do that, I'd consider three approaches.
- *An encrypted partition.* Rather than encrypting your entire hard disk, this uses whole-disk encryption tools like BitLocker to encrypt only a separate, non-boot partition on which you keep your data.
- *An encrypted vault.* This uses VeraCrypt to create an encrypted "vault" that, when in use, looks like a separate partition.
- *An encrypted cloud folder.* This uses a tool like BoxCryptor to perform file-by-file encryption of the contents of one or more folders on your machines. While intended to secure data you place in the cloud — you might even already be using it for that purpose — it secures that data on your machine as well. There's no requirement to use a cloud service to use BoxCryptor to encrypt data.

It's about more than your desktop

Everything I've just described applies to more than your computer at home. Yes, it could be stolen, but in reality, if you travel at all, there's a bigger risk.

Your laptop.

For a variety of reasons, an incredible number of laptops are lost or stolen each year. On each of those is data—often sensitive data—that the thief or finder can then access. (Thankfully, most do not, as they're more interested in reusing or reselling the hardware, but the risk of data exposure remains real.)

---

[119] https://veracrypt.fr/en/Home.html
[120] Yet another reason to ensure that you're backing up everything regularly.

At a minimum, the techniques I've described above should be considered for any laptop or mobile PC. Applying the same techniques to your computers at home will simply give you added security from the same types of threats.

What I do

What I've done has changed over the years.

Originally, I used TrueCrypt to create an encrypted vault on my laptop, and placed all of my data in it. This was convenient for a variety of reasons, mostly involving the ability to move data around on my various devices in pre-cloud days.

Today, I use a multi-pronged approach:
- I use BoxCryptor to secure the data I place in my DropBox folders. The side effect is that this data is also encrypted on all the computers on which I choose to place it.
- I use BitLocker whole-disk encryption on my laptop. This includes protecting myself by backing up data regularly and securing the encryption keys appropriately.
- While I don't currently, I have also used whole-disk encryption on my desktop.[121]

I'd also have no hesitation using VeraCrypt, TrueCrypt's supported successor, if a scenario called for it.

---

[121] Honestly, it was an oversight when I set up my current machine. I may turn it on at some point.

Part 5: Protect Your Online World

Is Using the Cloud Safe?

One of the comments I received on my article on lessons learned from a fairly public online hacking[122] was very concise:

"That's why the cloud is dangerous."

I think a lot of people feel that to varying degrees.

I disagree. *Strongly*.

I also think believing the cloud is dangerous prevents you from taking advantage of the things that the cloud can do for you—things like protecting your data.

It also misses the point that there are a number of things you're already doing "in the cloud", safely, and have been, for years.

What is "the cloud"?

I have to start by throwing away this silly, silly term, "the cloud." It's nothing more than a fancy marketing term. Ultimately, it has no real meaning.

The cloud is nothing more than services provided online over the internet.

Seriously, that's all it is.

Another way I saw it expressed recently was, "The cloud' is simply using someone else's computer."

Be it services that provide a place to store your data, enable you to communicate with others, provide applications, sell you things, or answer your technical questions, it's all happening in the cloud.

That's nothing new.

The cloud is new in name only

You've probably been using online services long before anyone thought to slap the name *cloud* on 'em.

- Do you have an online email account like Outlook.com or Gmail? You're keeping your email in the cloud.
- Do you use any kind of email? It gets from point "A" to point "B" through the cloud.
- Do you upload pictures to a photo-sharing site like Flickr, Picasa, or Photobucket? That's the cloud.
- Do you use an online backup service? You've been backing up to the cloud.

---

[122] https://askleo.com/103465

You get the idea.

I really, really want to drive home the point that this thing people are calling *the cloud* is nothing new. You've been using it already—probably for years before that silly name was attached to it.

So let's jettison the name and all the baggage comes with it, and call it what it really is: online services.

OK, fine. But is the cloud dangerous?

No more so now than it's ever been.

In fact, I'll claim that the average online service is becoming *safer* than ever before as service providers learn from mistakes and implement industry best practices.[123]

If anything has changed at all, it's the breadth of available online services and the number of people using them.

The fact is that any tool, when misused, can be dangerous.

For example, placing sensitive information in your online email account (and *only* your online email account), and then not using proper security on that account, is *absolutely* dangerous, and always has been. It's not that online email accounts are dangerous. The danger arises from *using them improperly*.

The same is true for any online service, be it those generating the latest buzz or those you've been using for years.

We're all at the mercy of service providers

At this point, many folks point out that the security breaches that we hear about are often the fault of, or related to, a problem at the provider of the service in question.

Many are, it's true.

But you know what? *That's not new either.*

---

[123] I don't have the data to back it up, but my feeling, based on being in this industry for as long as I have, is that by and large, service providers are getting better. The state of the art in online security is improving overall. If it seems like problems are happening more often, my sense is that it's simply because there are more online services now than there ever have been. My gut tells me that the number of failings as a percentage of available online services is going down.

As long as there have been service providers, there have been mistakes, breaches, and policy screw-ups at service providers.

I'm not (not! not! not!) trying to excuse service providers for making mistakes or screwing up. Every fiber of their corporate being should be working to prevent security-related errors, and mitigate the impact when they happen.

But the reality you and I have to deal with is that ultimately, service providers are staffed by humans, and humans make mistakes. Saying mistakes should never happen is unrealistic.

Worse, it's extremely poor security planning.

Besides, when it comes to security issues, we are most often our own worst enemies.

No one can protect you from you

Let's go back to the Mat Honan hack[124] for a moment, which is where the "the cloud is dangerous" comment originated.

Mat didn't lose his data because of the breaches he experienced.

Mat didn't lose his data because of problems with the online services (though there definitely were issues).

He lost his data because he wasn't backed up. Even if he had not been hacked, he was at high risk of losing everything anyway, had he lost his laptop or experienced a simple hard disk failure.

Had he been backing up his data, I'm betting there wouldn't have even been a news story.

On top of that, the hack reached as many of his accounts as it did because *he had linked all of his accounts together*. Mat helped the hackers get to his accounts.

No, the lesson here isn't that online services are dangerous. The lesson here is that *we have to assume responsibility for our own safety*.

And I'll say it once again: this is not new.

How to use online services safely

Using online services safely really boils down to not much more than the guidelines we've all heard before, plus maybe one or two new ones.

All, of course, augmented by a dose of common sense.
- Back up. If it's only in one place, it's not backed up.
- Use strong passwords, and set up and *keep current* all account recovery information[125]. Use extra security, such as two-factor authentication, if supported.

---

124 https://askleo.com/103465
125 https://askleo.com/15584

- Understand the security ramifications of using someone else's computer, or someone else using yours.
- Understand how to use internet connections provided by others securely, especially open Wi-Fi hotspots.[126]
- Don't link your important accounts together in such a way that breaching one opens the door to all of them; use different passwords (and perhaps even different email addresses) for each.
- Keep your software up to date, scan for malware, and all of the other items commonly listed to keep your computer safe on the internet.[127]

Only the part about using different email addresses for different accounts is relatively new—everything else should sound really, really familiar.

It really can be safe

To be clear, there's no such thing as perfect security[128], and that's true whether you keep your information securely locked away only on your own computer in your bedroom, or if you store it in the cloud. There's always something that can go wrong.

But by following basic security guidelines, there's no reason that most of the popular online services can't be used safely—at least as safely as the services you're already using.

Used properly, they can even *add* security by providing things like additional backups, throw-away email accounts, data replication, and more.

You do have to assume responsibility for your own security, and that includes not only taking reasonable precautions to prevent a problem, but also taking additional steps to minimize the impact should an issue arise.

Yes, you can avoid online services all together (just remember that means walking away from email as well), but you'd be missing out on so many of the opportunities the internet has to offer.

Rather than asking "Is the cloud dangerous?", learn to use it safely. You'll be much better off for it.

I know I am.

Postscript

Mat Honan, the victim of that public hacking I mentioned at the beginning, published an update detailing how he's recovered from his hacking.

One relevant quote that struck me: "I'm a bigger believer in cloud services than ever before."

---

[126] https://askleo.com/4790
[127] https://askleo.com/2374
[128] https://askleo.com/21748

This is the gentleman whose experience initiated this very discussion. While others are quick to blame "the cloud", after all is said and done, he's not one of them.

Neither am I.

Find his story at [Mat Honan: How I Resurrected My Digital Life After an Epic Hacking.](#)[129]

---

[129] https://go.askleo.com/honanrecovery

Back Up Your Email Using Thunderbird

Many years ago, I received a panic-stricken email from an individual whose account had been hacked. He had lost all access to the account and everything in it. His panic stemmed from the fact that, for whatever reason, the only copy of his master's thesis had been in that account.

It was gone, and there was no hope of recovery.[130]

Hopefully, you're not keeping something as important as a master's thesis only in your online email account. That's wrong on several levels. But I'm guessing there *are* things in your account that you never want to lose, such as photos, correspondence, or other things that you've exchanged in email.

The problem is, of course, that if it's only in your email account, it's not backed up.

Let's fix that. Let's back up your email.

Our example: Outlook.com and Hotmail

For this article, I'm going to use a Hotmail account—askleoexample@hotmail.com. I'll continue to access that account as I usually do, using the Outlook.com website, but we'll back it up to my PC using Thunderbird.

---

[130] My editor asked me, "If it was in his email account, he had either emailed it to someone or received it from somewhere else, so wasn't there hope of recovery after all?" — Perhaps. My assumption was it was probably saved as a draft email and hence never sent. Regardless, it was a bad way to "save" something, and by the time he came to me he'd apparently exhausted any options and hope for recovery.

The technique I'll use applies to almost all online accounts, including Gmail, Yahoo! and others. For this technique to work, the account must support a protocol called "IMAP". The good news is that IMAP is a common approach used to access email, and almost all email services support it.

In this example, I'll use Thunderbird as my desktop email program, but any desktop program that supports IMAP can back up your email, including Microsoft Office's Outlook and others.

Install Thunderbird

The first step is to download and install Thunderbird. Download Thunderbird[131] from the official download site here.[132]

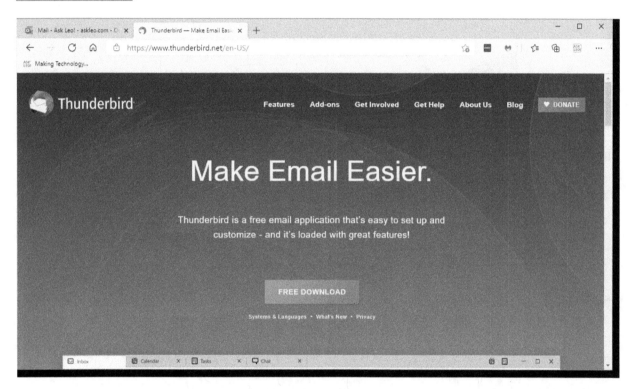

At this writing, the official URL is https://www.thunderbird.net.[133]

Download and run the Setup Wizard.

---

[131] It's critical that you download only from the official site. Do not get Thunderbird—or any software—from download sites or aggregators, unless explicitly instructed to by the official site. Almost all download sites now add unwanted software in addition to what you're looking for.
[132] https://www.thunderbird.net/en-US/
[133] https://www.thunderbird.net

The first choice is whether to accept the Standard settings or use Custom.

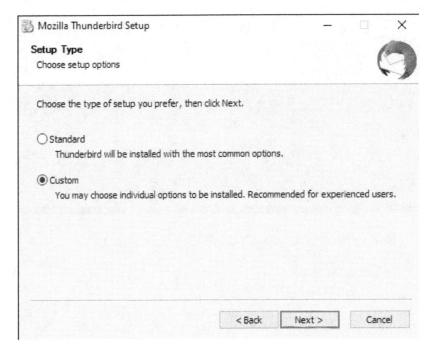

Always choose Custom. Even though we're going to accept all the suggestions made by the installer, choosing Custom is an important habit to get into to avoid malware and PUPs. Click Next through the subsequent settings and accept:

- Create icons on the Desktop, Start Menu and Quick Launch bar.
- The installation location for Thunderbird.

If there are additional options, read them carefully to make sure you understand what you are agreeing to.

Click **Install** on the last page of the Wizard to install Thunderbird.

When the installation is complete, leave "Launch Mozilla Thunderbird now" checked, and click on **Finish**.

Thunderbird may offer to import settings from another mail program if one is installed. Our goal here is to use Thunderbird simply for backup, so there's no need.

Configuring Thunderbird for a Hotmail account

When you first install Thunderbird, there are no email accounts configured. Thunderbird proceeds to the "Setup an Existing Account" dialog.

Enter your name, email address, and password. In my case, I'll enter "Ask Leo! - askleo.com" as my name, "askleoexample@hotmail.com" as my email address, and the password for that account.

Select **Remember password** if this computer is secure and you don't want to type in your password every time you fire up Thunderbird.

Click on Continue, and Thunderbird will consult its own database of email providers for the correct settings. Hotmail is in that database.

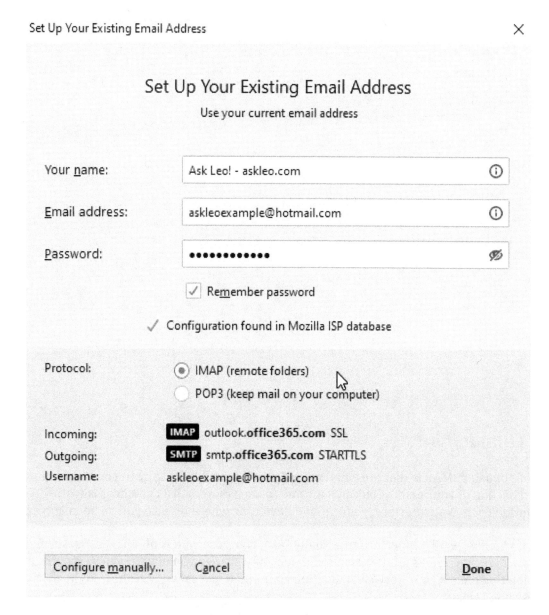

Make sure that IMAP is selected, and click **Done**.

If you have two-factor authentication enabled, you may be prompted by your email service to verify your identity or your sign-in will fail. You'll need to check with your provider for the technique to be used with a desktop email program. It typically involves creating what's called an "app password" to be used here instead of your normal password. You'll find more information here: I Enabled Two-Factor Authentication and Now My Email Program Can't Log In.

Thunderbird is now configured to access your Hotmail account and will begin downloading your mail.

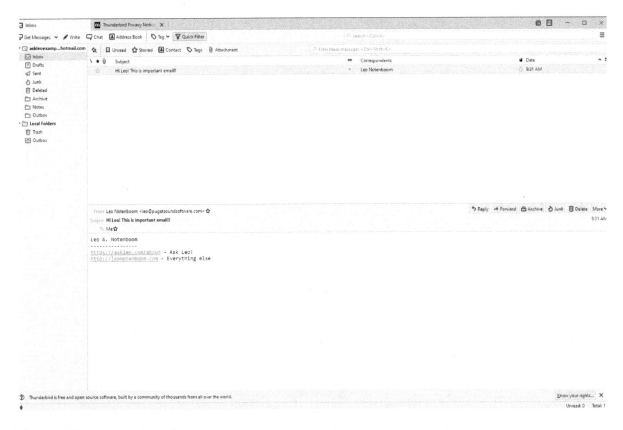

Using Thunderbird

The benefit of using IMAP is that the email program will download a copy to your computer, creating a backup of your email. You can continue to use your email as you normally do—typically via the Outlook.com web interface, your mobile device, or wherever else you've been accessing it.

You can, if you like, use Thunderbird to actually read, compose, and reply to messages. Email you read here will be marked as read elsewhere. In fact, any change you make, such as moving emails to folders, deleting emails, or otherwise managing your email messages, will show up in all the places you access your email.

Since IMAP mirrors the activity on your online account down to your PC, note that it will mirror any deletions as well. Delete a message online, and the next time you connect Thunderbird, the message will be deleted locally as well. Backing up your PC regularly[134] may provide you with an additional safety net, since the Thunderbird repository would be included in those backups as well.

Backing up contacts

To back up contacts, you need to manually export them from your email provider. Contacts are not included in the email protocol, and thus are not included in anything we've done so far.

Click on the contacts/people icon in the lower left of the Outlook.com display.

---

[134] Which you should be doing already anyway. Right?

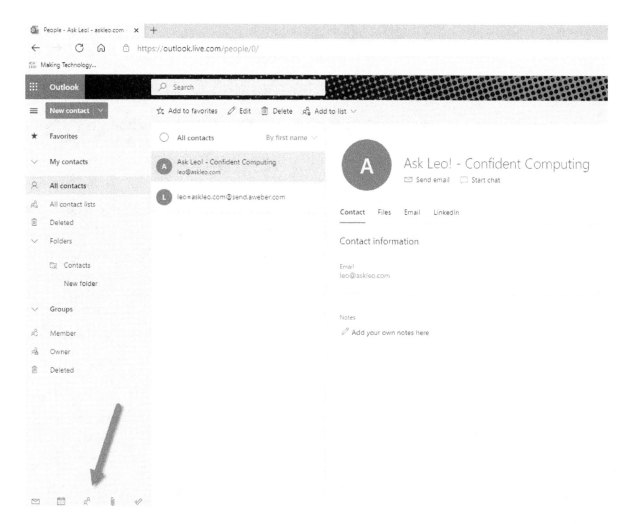

On the People page, click the **Manage** menu item, and then on **Export** contacts.

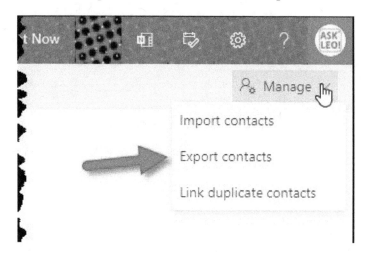

Save the downloaded file somewhere on your computer, ideally in a place that will also be backed up by your regular PC backups.

You can, if you like, import these contacts into Thunderbird, but since our goal here is to back them up, just downloading the file to our computer is enough.[135]

Back up your email

If you don't use Thunderbird regularly, it's important to run Thunderbird periodically to perform its backup. Once a day, once a week, or a couple of times a month, depending on how current you want your backup to be, run Thunderbird, and keep it running until it's downloaded a copy of all updates to your mail.

Similarly, since there's no automated download of your contacts, you'll need to do that regularly as well.

The good news here is that your email is backed up! Particularly when used in conjunction with ongoing PC backups, you're well protected against data loss due to account theft or other problems.

But, in all honesty, I still wouldn't keep the only copy of my master's thesis here. That's worth a few more copies in other locations for safekeeping.

---

135 Importing contacts from one service or program into another, while possible, is notoriously error prone and almost always results in some amount of lost data. This has to do with the lack of standards about what information is included in a "contact" and how that information should be represented.

How to Back Up Your Photos and Never Lose Them Again

Do you back up photos and video?

Everyone with a smartphone has a camera, and they're using 'em right and left to snap photos and shoot videos. Add in digital cameras from inexpensive to professional, and there's a *lot* of digital media being created every day.

Much of it isn't getting backed up. The goal? Multiple copies of your photos and videos in multiple places.

If it's in only one place, it's not backed up.

Back up photos on your digital camera

As soon as you take a picture or video with a digital camera, it exists in only one place: the original shot in the camera. It's impractical to back up after every shot, so we do have to accept a window of time where there's no backup at all. During that time, if you lose the camera, you lose all the photographs on it.

The best approach to minimize the window of vulnerability is to *copy* those photos to something else as soon as is convenient.

When I went on an overseas trip some years ago, I realized that the photographs I took would be the only thing truly irreplaceable should we run into trouble. So I developed this technique to back up photos:

- I took photographs throughout each day.
- At the end of the day, I *copied* those photographs to my laptop computer. Again, this is a *copy*, not a move. After this step, the photos were in *two* places: in the camera, and on my laptop.
- The laptop was also backed up each night to a portable external hard disk.[136] That resulted in *three* copies of the photos: the camera, the laptop, and the backup of the laptop. Only then would I consider removing the pictures from the camera's memory card.

---

[136] I actually took care to have the external hard disk travel as separately from the laptop as possible. For example, the camera was carry-on luggage, while the external hard drive was in checked baggage.

Given the importance of these photographs, I took an extra step. Rather than removing them from the camera's memory card, I physically mailed the memory card home as it filled up. They were waiting for me when I returned.

That last step might be overkill for day-to-day use, but something worth considering for those once-in-a-lifetime travel adventures, which this was.

The fundamental concept is very, very simple: as soon as is practical, make a second or third copy of the photographs stored on your camera on some other device, like your computer.

Back up photos and videos on your smartphone

Everything I've just outlined for your digital camera applies equally to your smartphone. Smartphones have the added convenience of being connected to the internet, which makes it easier. As soon as is practical, make a copy of the photographs and videos you've taken.

Sharing a photograph or video effectively makes a copy. This, then, is one simple way to back up: email your photographs to yourself. While still somewhat cumbersome, this gets us closer to being able to back up those photographs closer to the time that we take them. (Sharing on social media also makes a copy, but most reduce the quality of your upload, so you're not really backing up the original.)

Many cloud storage utilities, like DropBox, Microsoft's OneDrive, and others, will automatically upload photos and videos as you take them, if you give them permission to do so.[137]

This is exactly what I do on my phone. As soon as I take a photo, it's automatically uploaded to my DropBox account. That's one copy. It's then automatically downloaded to every computer I have running DropBox.

I *strongly* recommend this approach. Make sure you have enough storage in your online account, and make sure the application on your phone has permission to upload your photos. If there are size restrictions, consider lifting them. If there are network restrictions ("WiFi only", for example) consider lifting those as well. This way you'll know your photos will be backed up as soon as you take them.

If you must leave restrictions in place, make sure items not backed up automatically get backed up some other way as soon as possible.

Back up photos to your cloud

Many times, photographs or videos posted using mobile apps like Facebook, Instagram, Twitter, and others, is posted directly online. This implies it exists in only one place: online. That means it's

---

[137] In fact, many get quite insistent, and it's easy to have multiple utilities all trying to do it for you.

not backed up. For example, if you lose access to your account, you'll lose all the images you've stored there.

This is important.
- Understand how the app works. Does it leave a copy of the photo on your device? If so, great: you can back it up using the techniques I've outlined above.[138]
- If the app only uploads to their service, you'll need to back it up yourself. As soon as it's convenient, make a copy. Download the image or video to your PC, or share it to a different service or via email.
- Consider not using the app's own camera feature. Instead, take pictures using the camera app on your device, which is backed up by your cloud storage service. Then share the specific photo or video to, or open it with, the social media app you intend to use.

Cloud services—particularly video- and photo-specific services—can be extremely helpful in sharing or backing up your images. They often serve both functions. But *you must be aware* of how they work. You need to take the right steps so as not to leave your photos in only one place that you might then lose forever.

Now that they're on your PC, back that up too

The techniques above ultimately result in your photos and videos making their way to your PC—either manually, as you copy images from your camera or online account, or automatically, as a cloud sync service does it for you.

That's still not quite enough.

Naturally, you should be backing up your computer, and for more reasons than just your pictures. If you've got a properly configured periodic backup that includes the folders in which you store your photos and videos, you're pretty close to being done. In fact, in most cases, you can probably stop here.

But I want you to consider one more option: backing up your photos and videos to the cloud—again, if you've followed my advice in the previous section.

The problem is that for many people, these photos and videos are precious memories that can never be replaced if lost. If anything warrants an additional layer of protection, these photos qualify. By backing up to an online service, you're protected from anything that might take out your home computer(s) and backup(s), like a fire or a burglary.

I'd consider either of two approaches:
- Use a photo-sharing service, like Flickr, Picasa, or others, and upload everything. You may not need to make everything publicly visible—in fact, you probably don't want to—but you'll have backup copies of everything in one place, optimized for review (and, if you choose, sharing as well).

---

[138] Many of the DropBox-like services notice that certain apps are installed or that certain folders exist, and may offer to upload the photos taken in those apps in addition to those taken by the device's camera app.

- Use an online backup service. Images and videos are just files on your computer, and all of the online backup services are tailored to back up whatever data you might choose to include. Using an online service might be preferable if you're already using one to back up your computer, or you realize that there are a few more things that fall into the "too precious to lose" category besides images.

In all cases, I strongly encourage you to, *at a minimum*, save the original, highest resolution, un-edited versions of your files. You can always re-create the edited versions if you elect not to save them as well, but you can't go back to the original from a modified, cropped, tweaked, or resized file.

A note about those "sensitive" photos

When I wrote the original version of this article, news broke of a hacker who gained access to a number of celebrity nude photos. He'd hacked into their iCloud accounts.

Please think carefully before taking "sensitive" photos (not limited to naked selfies). The safest thing to do is not take photos or videos that would embarrass or harm you if posted publicly.

I realize that's not always possible. Sometimes taking a photo of something sensitive is exactly the right thing to do, for any number of reasons.

If you find yourself in this situation, you need to take extra care to avoid accidental disclosure.
- *Think twice about sharing.* If it can be seen, it can be copied. When you share a photo or video with a friend, you lose all control over it. Some day -- perhaps when they are no longer your friend -- they could post it publicly.
- *Remove it from the cloud.* I still strongly recommend using cloud services to back up your photos on devices that support it. In the case of sensitive information, I *also* strongly recommend later moving that back-up copy to local storage over which you have more control.
- *If stored on line, encrypt it.* If you do use cloud services for backup, make sure those backups are encrypted. This means you can't use them as an easy source for sharing, but that's exactly what you want: to keep private things private.
- *Remove it from the camera.* Many people's sensitive photographs are compromised by nothing more complicated than losing their smartphone or camera. Even if it's quickly recovered, the information on the device can be copied.

Much of this applies to any sensitive information, including emails and documents stored in an online account. Photographs and videos, however, seem to be a particularly ripe spot for hacker activity.

How Do I Backup My WordPress Site?[139]

We've looked at how important it is to back up your computer, your email, and your photos, but there is one aspect of your online life that is easily overlooked when it comes to backing up.

This is specifically for folks who have websites. Perhaps you have one for your personal blog, business, or organization.

If you do, there's a good chance it runs WordPress, the content management software behind a surprisingly large number of websites, including Ask Leo!.

If your web host and site were to completely disappear overnight, would that be a problem?

I thought so.

The goal

It seems over-the-top, doesn't it? How often do web hosts just suddenly disappear and go out of business, after all?

It's happened. I've had to pick up the pieces.

More importantly, by protecting yourself against this ultimate catastrophe, you'll be protected against everything else that can go wrong.

The goal here is simple: to be able to restore your site to a completely different web host, and have it back up and running as it was before—quickly.

Relying on your host

The first reaction of many is to confirm that their web host is backing up their server.

However:
- Many are not; backups are your responsibility.
- Many are, but only for "server level" issues like hard disk failures. If you have a software (i.e. WordPress) problem, you might not have access to those backups.
- Many are, but will only restore your site in an all-or-nothing fashion. If you're just attempting to recover an accidentally deleted file, you have to decide if it's worth overwriting your entire site with a previous backup.

---

[139] Based on an article originally taken from Ask Leo! On Business – https://biz.askleo.com.

- Some do exactly as we need: easily accessible backups we can restore, completely or partially, as needed.

Of course, if your host is the problem – as in it just disappeared completely – they'll have taken their backups with them.

So, yes, make sure your host is providing backups of some form, and take the time to understand exactly how they may or may not be useful. They could be the most expedient solution to a future problem.

But then do more.

BackupBuddy

I'm a big fan of the WordPress plugin BackupBuddy. It's not free, but it does everything I expect.

There are two distinct components to a WordPress site:
- Files. By that I mean the WordPress files themselves: the themes, plugins, and media files you've uploaded to the site.
- Data. All of your content—the articles, comments, and the configuration of your site—is stored in a database separate from your files.

Each is important. Backing up both is essential.

Backing up your site and storing the backup on the website's server isn't enough. Once again, should your web host suddenly disappear, your server, and any backups it contains, will also disappear.

BackupBuddy allows you to schedule automated backups and store those backups elsewhere. You can place your backups either in BackupBuddy's own storage (called "Stash"), or services like Google Drive, Dropbox, or others. Or you can download a zip file every so often.

BackupBuddy can also help move a WordPress site to a completely different domain (for example, moving the site and its content from "askleo.com" to "somerandomservice.com" —a very complex process). That's how I was introduced to the plugin.

When disaster strikes

The goal is to be able to restore your website on a completely new host in the absolute worst-case scenario.

With BackupBuddy, that's pretty simple: upload a bootstrapping script provided by BackupBuddy, point it at your backup, and after a couple of configuration steps, the process restores your site.

Assuming you've changed your domain's DNS to point to your new web host, you're done, at least with respect to your website.

Less than major catastrophes

Perhaps more importantly, though, that ".zip" file created by BackupBuddy contains everything in and on your site.

That means you (or someone helping you) can extract anything you need, at any time. Delete a file accidentally? Recover it from the backup. Need to revert to an old copy of an uploaded image? It's in there.

Need one of your articles back? It's in there too, in the included backup of the database.

What about export?

WordPress has an Export option in its Tools that can be used for backup—sort of.

The Export function is, indeed, a fine way to make a copy of your content, but it's important to realize that it exports only your content. Everything else—your site's plugins, themes, configuration, settings, and more—is not included.

The reason it's a viable, better-than-nothing backup is that everything not included can be reinstalled, re-setup, and re-configured. It may take time—perhaps even lots of it—but it's generally possible.

Your content, however, is what makes your site unique. If you're not going to go the BackupBuddy route, then at a minimum, back up your content by exporting it every so often. Include the downloaded file in the regular backups of your PC.

Start backing up now

It's not a stretch to say that a well-crafted website is an incredible asset to a company or cause.

It's also not a stretch to say that the sudden disappearance of a website that isn't backed up can cause no end of grief to that company or cause. It can even lead to its own sudden disappearance.

It's something I'll be saying for a long, long time: back up.

Particularly if you've invested time and resources into your site, it's time to start backing up.

Your Six Strongest Practical Password Techniques, Ranked

My most memorable password accessed a status terminal in the computer center at school. I don't recall the account ID, but after 40+ years I can still remember that the password was iforgot.

A very memorable and horrible password.

It was appropriate at the time because it was a public-access terminal — anyone could sign in — and for some reason, a password of some sort was required. They made it simple and even had it posted on the terminal itself.

There was zero security.

You want something better. There are a number of techniques to generating strong passwords. I'll review some, from best to worst.

My criteria

These are my personal opinions and are based on the last 18+ years of helping people with their passwords.

My criteria are simple:
- Passwords must be able to resist automated brute-force "try every password" attacks.
- Passwords must be very unguessable.
- Passwords must be extremely unlikely to have been encountered anywhere else.

In some cases, it would also be nice if they were easy to memorize.

I'm ruling out some of the more esoteric approaches, even though they might be secure, because it's important these techniques be practical as well as secure.

My assumptions

I strongly recommend using two-factor authentication, but the ranking below assumes you're not. While adding two-factor doesn't change my ranking, in some ways it minimizes the differences in security between approaches.

I assume you're not going to use the same password on multiple sites, *period*. That's one of the most dangerous security practices, regardless of the strength of your passwords.

I assume you're using a password vault of some sort. While being able to remember some passwords might be nice, it's just not practical when using strong, long, passwords that are different for every account. This is one of the reasons that I and so many others strongly recommend using password vaults: they enable the use of strong passwords on different sites without taxing your memory or your patience.

#1: Long random characters

Password: **SBH2F%b^xDCUQf5frqBR**

The strongest approach is the one you may be most afraid of: long strings of completely random characters. The example above is a 20-character password generated by LastPass. There are many other tools that generate passwords for you, and many also let you control what kinds of characters are used.

Since not all special characters can be used on all systems, my own default configuration is to use 20-character passwords without special characters. At 20 characters, that's more than sufficiently strong.

Using 20 random-character passwords is considered so strong that the length doesn't even appear on many "how long would it take to crack" password reports. The last report I looked at topped out at 14—and that took 968 *centuries* to crack using a large distributed system (perhaps a very large botnet). My recommendation of 20-character passwords is future-proof, and possible because I use a password vault.

#2: Long with multiple random words

Password: **drying karen ruth afoot sauce**

We all remember "correct horse battery staple" from the XKCD cartoon.[140] That shows you just how memorable words can be. If you can build a picture (as the cartoon describes) of some nonsense scenario involving randomly selected words, all the better to help you recall it without any aid.

Our example—a 29-character password created by five completely random words—is great. A five-random-word password would take a large distributed system of many computers 14 years to crack. That seems plenty secure. (Include spaces if you're so inclined and the service supports it. If not running them all together is also a fine approach: "dryingkarenruthafootsauce", or perhaps capitalize instead: "DryingKarenRuthAfootSauce".)

This is a good solution for passwords you must remember—perhaps the password to your password vault itself.

I use a slightly less secure variation described below.

#2a: Long with multi-word mangled phrases

Password: **Obi-Wan you're my only soap**

---

[140] https://xkcd.com/936/

That's memorable, and at 27 characters, it's plenty long to defeat brute force attacks. It's a slight mangling of a phrase that's <u>well known in pop culture</u>.[141]

What makes it secure against guessing is the mangling: it starts two words into the phrase, drops one word, and includes a word not in the original. If that doesn't seem mangled enough for you (though I believe it is), you can certainly do more to obfuscate the actual words used while maintaining the memorableness of the phrase. Just remember how you mangle it.

I use this technique for passwords I need to remember. I have a specific phrase and the techniques I used to mangle it memorized.

There are many variations of this technique. For example, using the first letter of each apparently random word to spell out a memorable keyword. Remembering *kitten* might be the doorway to help you remember your password as "kitten incite Tuesday tornado else nothing".

#3: Medium-length words with padding

Password: ***-*-*breakfast pancakes*-*-***

Length trumps just about everything when creating a password resistant to brute-force cracking. So a combination of random or semi-random words with some standard padding can end up being quite secure.

The example here is a password made up of two common words with padding added before and after. In this case, the padding is a pattern. Adding an easily recalled padding pattern to a password or passphrase is a useful technique.

At 28 characters, this password is not going to be brute-forced, and while "breakfast pancakes" might be a word pattern used in some password guessers, adding a pattern of your own creation thwarts that as well.

#4: Medium-length random characters

Password: **l)ws7.BOZ1**

This is nothing more than our #1 technique, but shorter: 10 characters instead of 20. This technique creates a "good" password that would take nine years to crack using a multi-computer attack. You can, of course, adjust the length as you see fit, but for a truly random selection, I would not go below 10 characters.

As a variation that's easier to type, a 12-character password using only upper and lower case alphanumeric characters (example: "qqkCapnm5Jx7") would take 24 years to crack.

---

[141] https://knowyourmeme.com/memes/help-me-obi-wan-kenobi-youre-my-only-hope

This approach is why my current recommendation for basic passwords is 12 random characters or longer, giving you the flexibility to make it easy to type by eliminating special characters if you want.

#5: Shorter with padding

Password: ***4*iforgot*4***

I keep coming back to length and padding as great ways to make those old passwords you remember so easily much more secure. In this example, I've taken that memorable but horrible password I used 40 years ago and made it significantly more secure by adding a simple pattern of my own creation before and after. It's now a good, secure, 13-character password.

#6: Shorter random characters

Password: **(8dQ,]qa**

If you must use a password less than 12 characters in length—as, unbelievably, some older systems still require—then your only secure option is to use passwords of completely random characters, including letters, numbers, upper and lower case, and special characters.

This is your "least bad" option under those constraints.

Making it easier

I will continue to beat the drum for using a password manager for two very important reasons:
- It makes using the most secure techniques for password generation easy.
- It makes using a different password on every site easy.

Add two-factor authentication for additional security wherever possible, but regardless, use the strongest passwords you possibly can.

How Long Should a Password Be?

For a long time, the common thinking was that the best, most practical passwords consisted of a random combination of upper and lower-case letters, numbers, and a special character or two. If so composed, password length needed to be only eight characters.

Randomness remains important, but as it turns out, size matters more.

A password today should have a minimum of 12 characters, and ideally, 16 or even more.

Large-scale account hacks

When you hear about large numbers of accounts being stolen by a hack at some service provider, you are naturally concerned that the hacker may now have access to your account names and passwords. If the service was storing your *actual* passwords, that could indeed be the case. (As I've said before, if a service is storing your *actual* passwords[142], they simply don't understand security or they have made some horrifically bad decisions.)

In fact, most services store an encrypted (technically, a "hashed") form of your password. For example, if my password were "password" (and that's a very poor password, of course), then a service might store

5e884898da28047151d0e56f8dc6292773603d0d6aabbdd62a11ef721d1542d8

—the hash value that corresponds to that password. [143]

What that means is that hackers do *not* get a list of user names and passwords. What they get is a list of usernames and password *hashes*.

And what's great about hashes is that you can calculate a hash from a password, but you cannot do the reverse—*you cannot calculate the password from the hash.*

As a result, one would think that by being hashed it'd be pretty unhackable, right?

Sadly, not so much.

Dictionary attacks

The most common type of password attack is simply a high-speed guessing game. This doesn't work on an actual log-in page;[144] they're slow, and will quickly deny further access after too many attempts. But this technique works wonderfully if the hacker has the entire database of account and password hashes sitting on his computer.

---

[142] If they can respond to an "I forgot my password" request with your *actual, current* password, then they have stored your password. This is bad. Best practice is to reset it to something new, either via a reset link, or by emailing a new password to you *exactly once*, after which the service no longer has it.
[143] For the technically curious, I'm using an un-salted sha256 as the hashing function here. That's technically better than md5 or sha1 that's commonly used.
[144] https://askleo.com/14547

These attacks involve starting with an exhaustive list of possible words and known common passwords (including names, profanities, acronyms, and more) and perhaps a few rules to try interesting and common ways that people try to obfuscate words. They calculate the hash of each guess, and if it matches what was found in the compromised database of account information that they're working against, they've figured out the password for that account.

As we'll see in a moment, it's easy for hackers to make an amazing number of guesses is a short amount of time.

That's why you're not using a short password, or using common obfuscations, right?

That's why a password created from a totally random combination of characters is best. It forces hackers to move on to a true brute force attack of every possible combination to gain access.

Brute force attacks

Computers are fast. In fact, the computer on your desk is so fast that its ability to do simple operations is measured in terms of *billions* of operations per second.

Creating a password hash is not a simple operation, on purpose. However, it's still something that can be done very quickly on most machines today. Spread the work over a number of machines—perhaps a botnet—and the amount of processing power that can be thrown at password cracking is amazing.

The net impact is that it's now feasible to calculate the encrypted hash values for *all possible eight-character passwords* comprised of upper and lowercase alphabetic characters and digits.

Sixty-two possible characters (26 lower case, 26 upper case, 10 digits), in each of the eight positions gives us 221,919,451,578,090,[145] or over 221 trillion, combinations.[146]

This seems like a lot, until you realize that an off-line attack (which is easily performed once you've stolen a database of usernames and encrypted passwords) can be completed in a few hours. (This assumes technology which can "guess" something like 10 billion passwords per second—which, for those performing these kinds of attacks, is quite possible.)

It doesn't matter what your password is; if it's eight characters and constructed using upper and lower case letters and numbers, the hackers now have it—even if it was hashed by the service they stole it from.

---

[145] OK, OK. Technically, the number is actually 221,919,451,578,090 + 3,579,345,993,194 + 57,731,386,986 + 931,151,402 + 15,018,570 + 242,234 + 3,844 + 62. Then we also add in the possibilities of seven-character passwords, six, five, four, and so on. I'm not doing the math. It's around 225 trillion.

[146] Many of the numbers and attack estimates here come from or are based on GRC.com's excellent Password Haystack page. Included there are links to an excellent *Security Now!* podcast discussing password length and how size really does matter.

Why 12 is better and 16 better still

As we've seen, eight-character passwords give you over 221 trillion combinations, which can be reasonably brute-force guessed offline in hours.

Twelve characters give you over three sextillion (3,279,156,381,453,603,096,810). The offline brute-force guessing time in this case would be measured in *centuries.*

Sixteen takes the calculation off the chart. Today.

That's why 16 is better than 12, and both are better than eight.

What about special characters?

I did leave out special characters.

Let's say that the system you're using allows you to use any of 10 different "special characters" in addition to A-Z, a-z, and 0-9. Now, instead of 62 characters, we have 72 possibilities per position.

That takes us to 700 trillion possibilities for an eight-character password.

Compared to sticking with the original 62 letters and numbers, adding only a single "normal" character makes a nine-character password significantly more secure.

That takes us to over 13 *quadrillion* possibilities.

Yes, adding special characters makes your password better, but significantly better *yet* is to simply add one more character.

So add two. Or six. ☺

Long passwords are good; passphrases are better

The difference is really a semantic one, but in general:
- A password is a random string of characters.
- A passphrase is a longer string of words.

Why pass*phrase*? Because they're easier to remember, so it's easier to make longs—and as we saw, password length is perhaps the single easiest way to increase the security of a password.

"BT6aKgcAN44VK4yw" is a very nice, secure 16-character password that's difficult to remember. In fact, the only way to use this is with a password manager that remembers it for you.

Pass-phrase:
Its fleece was white as you know nothing John Snow

On the other hand, "Its fleece was white as you know nothing John Snow", at 50 characters, is wonderfully long, secure, and most of all, *memorable*. Much like the now-canonical example of "Correct Horse Battery Staple", you may even have a difficult time forgetting it.[147]

The biggest problem with passphrases? Many services that use passwords don't allow spaces or such lengthy passwords.

Shouldn't services fix this and do better?

Absolutely, they should. And many do.

As I've stated above, passwords shouldn't be kept in plain text anywhere by the service at all ... yet some do.

There are techniques that make brute-force attacks significantly harder — and yet, many use techniques that are *easier* than the example above.

There are services that do a great job of keeping your information secure. There are also services that don't. The problem is that you really can't be certain which is which.

To be safe, you have to act like they're all at risk.

The bottom line

The bottom line for staying safe is simply this:
- *Don't trust that the service* you're using is handling passwords properly. While many do, it's painfully clear that many do not, and you won't know which kind you're dealing with until it's too late.
- *Use longer passwords*: 12 characters minimum, 16 if at all possible.
- *Use even longer passphrases* where they're supported, or where information is particularly sensitive.
- *Use a different password* for each different site login you have. That way, a password compromised on one service won't give hackers access to everything else.[148]

Even the best eight-character passwords should no longer be considered secure. Twelve is "good enough for now," but you really should consider moving to 16 for the long run.

---

[147] Particularly if you're a *Game of Thrones* fan. ☺ And yes, I know that John Snow is actually Jon Snow. That's another level of handy, yet easy to remember, obfuscation.
[148] https://askleo.com/11788

Why is It So Important to Use a Different Password for Everything?

> **"**
> *I keep hearing I'm supposed to use a different password on every internet site where I have an account. What a pain! I can't remember all of those passwords. Yeah, I know. You want me to use a password manager thing, but that seems like putting a bunch of really important things into a single basket. What if that basket gets hacked? I use a strong password, why isn't that enough?*

I'm sorry, but a single strong password just isn't enough anymore. You must use *different* strong passwords on every site where you have an account—at least, every important site.

And yes, you must devise a way to manage them all.

Let me run down an example scenario that's causing all of this emphasis on multiple different passwords.

The all-too-common scenario

The scenario I'm about to describe is very common. While the specifics won't apply to you exactly, it'll conceptually illustrate what can happen.

Let's say you have an account at some online service—I'll call it Service A. In addition, you have a Yahoo! account because you use Flickr, a Google account because you use Gmail and a number of other Google services, a Microsoft account because you have Windows, and we'll throw in a Dropbox account because you've been listening to me recommend it. You probably have other accounts I haven't listed here, but you get the idea. You have lots of accounts to a number of online services.

You have a wonderfully strong password that you've memorized: 16 completely random characters. Maybe something like 24rZFPI69u$c%*jr.

And you use that same wonderfully strong password *everywhere*.

Here's how it can go horribly, horribly wrong.

Anatomy of a hack

Service A has the best of intentions, but honestly, they don't "get" security. Perhaps they store passwords in their database in plain text, allowing anyone with access to see them. They do that because it's easy, it's fast, and it allows them to solve the problem quickly. They make the assumption that the database containing your password will be impenetrable.

Hackers *love* it when site designers make assumptions like that because, of course, the assumption is incorrect.

One day, a hacker breaches site security and steals a copy of the customer/user database. The hacker walks away with a database that contains the following information for every user:

- Their log-in ID
- The email address associated with the account
- The password (or enough information from which the password can be determined)[149]
- Password hints

They can log in to your account on Service A. That may or may not be a big deal, depending on what Service A is and how you use it.

But it opens a very dangerous door.

It doesn't have to be a hack

It's important to understand that while this example centers around what we hear about in the news most often—the hack of an online service and the theft of their user database—it's certainly not limited to that.

Essentially, anything that could compromise your password brings you to this point. That includes:
- Sharing it with the wrong person.
- Keyloggers and other malware sniffing your password as you type it in.
- Improper use of an open Wi-Fi hotspot.

And so on.

Anything that puts your single password into the hands of a malicious individual puts you at greater risk than you might assume.

Password skeet shooting

Once they have your password, the hackers go hunting.

As most people have accounts on one or more of the major services I mentioned, the hackers start trying the information from Service A as if it were the correct information for Gmail, Outlook.com, Yahoo, Facebook, Twitter, Dropbox, and more.

They try your email address and password to log in to the email service you're using.

They try your log-in ID and password (or that email address and password) on as many other services as they can.

And very often, *it works.* The hackers gain access to another account of yours that was completely unrelated to the initial security breach.

---

[149] Thankfully, services rarely store the actual password—though of course they could. (If your service can tell you your actual password, then they're doing it wrong, and they've stored the password itself somewhere). Rather, they store what's called a "hash" of the password. Depending on several factors— typically, poor decisions made by whoever implemented the authentication mechanism—it is occasionally possible for hackers to indirectly reverse-engineer passwords from hashes.

Unrelated, of course, except that you used the same password at both.

If you use the same password everywhere, a single leak of that password puts all your accounts at risk. Hackers will be able to log in to your other online accounts as well.

OK, maybe not all; maybe only a few. But a few is all it takes.

The weakest link

Note that this has absolutely nothing to do with the security expertise of the sites where your account is eventually compromised. Gmail, Outlook.com, Yahoo, and others have excellent security, but that fact doesn't factor into this scenario at all.

Service A was the weakest link. *Their* security wasn't up to the task. Their database was breached. Their information was leaked. Your account information and password—the password you use everywhere—was exposed.

Service A was at fault.

But the real problem is your use of that single password everywhere.

It shouldn't be this way

I'll happily admit that things like this shouldn't happen.

But they do. Not terribly often, but often enough.

And most services are better at security than our fictional Service A.

But it's also not a black-or-white equation. Even large corporations that either should know better or simply miss things can put your information at risk. For example, a hack at Adobe a couple of years ago had the potential to expose the passwords of 130 million Adobe account holders.[150]

I hate to say you can't trust anyone, but ultimately, you shouldn't trust anyone not to accidentally expose your password.

And, as I mentioned above, it doesn't have to be a big service breach for there to be a problem.

Using a different password on each site limits your exposure if any of those sites are compromised.

Managing lots of passwords

So it comes down to how to manage a lot of different (and long and complex) passwords.

I still recommend LastPass and use it myself.

Doesn't that put all my eggs in one basket?

---

[150] https://go.askleo.com/adobe_blunder

Yes, it does, but it's a very good basket. And I've taken additional steps to ensure that it stays that way.

I talk about LastPass in more depth in <u>LastPass—Securely keep track of multiple passwords on multiple devices</u>,[151] but I'll highlight two important reasons I consider LastPass secure:

- The people at LastPass don't know your master password. They couldn't tell you what it is if they wanted to. They cannot access your data at all; all they can see is the encrypted data. Even if a hacker were to somehow <u>gain access to their databases</u>,[152] the hacker would also be unable to decrypt and view your information, because LastPass does encryption right. Decryption happens locally on your machine, so the only thing ever transmitted between your computer and LastPass is the encrypted data.
- Of course I use a strong password. But LastPass also supports two-factor authentication, and I've enabled it on my account. If you somehow got my master password, you'd still need my second factor in your possession to be able to unlock my LastPass vault.

Ultimately, it's up to you. There are several password managers out there, but LastPass is the one I trust.

The very short bottom line

My recommendation remains:

- Use long, strong passwords. Twelve {{At the beginning you mention 16; do you want to change it here too?}}characters minimally, ideally more, and randomly generated (there are several random-generator tools available, including one in LastPass). Alternately, and if allowed, use a passphrase at least four words long, ideally with spaces.
- Use a different password for every log-in account you have. *Every one.*
- Use a password manager like LastPass to keep track of them all for you.
- Use a strong password or pass*phrase* on LastPass itself.
- Consider enabling two-factor authentication on LastPass for additional security of that very important basket of information.

---

[151] https://askleo.com/5744
[152] https://askleo.com/5343

Why Password Managers are Safer than the Alternatives

> " *Recently I tried to use RoboForm for an account at a large financial institution, but I couldn't get it to work. In response to my inquiry, this institution said they do not permit log in using credentials that are stored on software because the security of the password could become jeopardized if my computer were hacked, invaded, etc. Is this true? Am I safer not to use tools like RoboForm?*

There are people who believe that using password managers represents a single point of failure. Very technically, they are correct: if someone gains access to your password manager, they have access to everything within it.

Not so technically, I strongly believe they are misguided.

Using a password manager is, in my opinion, *significantly* safer than the alternatives.

Security best practices

Without using a password manager, the idea is that you:
- Have good, strong passwords (long and complex).
- Keep them nowhere but in your head (memorable).
- Use a different password on every site or service that requires one (unique).

Yes, that would be ideal.

Without using a password manager, it's also completely impractical.

Those requirements simply can't all be met at the same time. At least one, if not two, will be compromised without the aid of a password vault.

Without a password manager

Without a password manager, you'll compromise your security in some way.
- You'll choose a less secure, easy-to-remember password (short and/or not complex).
- You'll use the same password at multiple sites (not unique).
- You'll save the password using technology that is not secure (not memorable).

Any one of those can significantly compromise your security.

With a password manager

Password managers make best practices trivially easy.
Using a password manager allows you to:

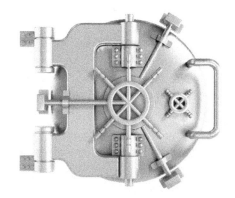

- Generate and use secure, complex, and appropriately long passwords.
- Never need to type or remember passwords— the password manager remembers them for you.
- Use different passwords on different sites.

These are things that people *don't* do unless they have a tool in place to help them. Password managers are specifically designed to do exactly that securely.

Most password managers add several features that make improved security even more convenient. They can:

- Synchronize your information across multiple computers.
- Be used on mobile devices.
- Automatically fill in not just passwords, but common web forms.
- Securely store other information of many types.

And they do all of that with more security than almost all alternatives..

If you're compromised, you're compromised

It is true that if your computer is compromised, all bets are off. Malware *could* gain access to whatever it is you have stored on the computer.

For example, while I'm logged into LastPass, all the information is technically available to software running on my machine—good software or bad.

That's a serious concern, and not to be taken lightly.

But it's a concern that exists *regardless of whether you use a password manager or not.* All bets are off if a keylogger captures what you enter when you log in to your bank account.

Avoiding a password manager doesn't increase your security one whit.

But are password managers safe?

Yes. Password managers are safer than any practical alternative.

There are no absolutes -- that, too, is a practical reality. There is no such thing as absolute security.[153] As I said earlier, if you fall victim to malware, all bets are off, no matter what technique(s) you use.

Password managers are the safest way to keep a record of your online account information, but they are no safer than:
- The master password you use to access the password manager.
- Your own ability to use your computer safely.[154]

The last one scares most people, but my claim is that using password managers is, in fact, one way to use your computer more safely.

What I do

I keep my machine(s) secure by doing the traditional things that you hear over and over:[155] keeping software up-to-date, running up-to-date scans, avoiding malicious websites and downloads, not falling for phishing, and so on and so on.

I use LastPass[156] to manage my passwords and additional security information.

I use Google Authenticator, a form of two-factor authentication, to access my LastPass vault. You can't get in to my LastPass account *even if you know my master password*. To get access to my LastPass vault, you need both my master password *and* my mobile phone.

I have LastPass automatically log out after some amount of time on any device which I'm not 100% certain won't get stolen or accessed without my permission.

I keep my master password secure and complex.[157]

I back up my LastPass vault[158] regularly.

I'm not going to claim it's impossible for anything bad to happen -- that'd be a foolish claim. I am, however, very satisfied with the risks and trade-offs, and absolutely convinced that using LastPass (or any reputable password manager) keeps me as safe as possible, and safer than not using one at all.

Let's face it: even doing business *offline* has risks and trade-offs.

---

[153] https://askleo.com/16029
[154] https://askleo.com/2374
[155] https://askleo.com/2374
[156] https://askleo.com/5744
[157] https://askleo.com/5440
[158] https://askleo.com/9181

How Two-Factor Authentication Works

We rely on passwords to protect our online world. At the same time, hackers seem to be getting better at figuring them out.

In response, security folks created something called "two-factor" or "multi-factor" authentication, which uses two different types of information. Both must be correct to prove you are who you say you are and give you access to the account.

It's something I *strongly* suggest you use. Two-factor authentication keeps your account secure even if your password is compromised.

Authentication

When we talk about security and passwords and the like, the word "authentication" gets thrown around a lot.

All authentication means is proving that you are who you say you are. It's validates you are *authentically* you, and not some impostor.

It's important, because once you've shown you are who you say you are, you have the right to use the things that are yours. Once you prove you are you, for example, you're allowed to access your email account.

In person, we can use physical things, like a photo ID, to prove we are who we say we are. Online, things get more difficult.

What you know, and what you have

Authentication has almost always been in the form of *something you know*. You know your username and the password that goes with it. Since only you should know your password, your ability to type it in proves you must be you and no one else.

If you forget your password, the answers to a set of security questions might be used instead, which still boil down to something(s) you—and hopefully only you[159]—know.

Something you know is easy to transfer from one person to another. When it's on purpose, that's okay, albeit it less than secure. When someone who shouldn't know your password learns it, something *you* know becomes something *they* know, too. The result? They can impersonate you, too.

---

[159] Since we've made so much of our information public in recent years, these questions have fallen out of favor. Too many other people might be able to discover the answers to your so-called "secret" questions.

What you have

Two-factor authentication typically adds something you have to how you prove you are you. When it comes time to authenticate, you need two things:

- Something you know: you must know your username and the password that only you should know.
- Something you have: you must possess something specific that is also completely unique to only you.

How you go about *proving* you have something in your possession is pretty hard to do securely—until you factor in encryption. For example "what you have" might be a smartphone running an application that has been associated with your account using encryption. More on that in a moment.

What you are

There's an additional factor sometimes combined with a password, and sometimes even a password plus something you have:[160] something you *are*.

Most commonly, this is biometric data like your fingerprint or your face, each of which is, in theory, unique to you. When it comes time to authenticate, you need two things:

- *Something you know*: you must know your username and the password that only you should know.
- *Something you are*: you must provide your fingerprint or allow a facial scan, those things again being completely unique to you.

Fingerprint and face ID are fairly common of late, though it's generally used by itself as a single factor. Only when combined with *something you know* and/or *something you have* is it considered multi-factor.

Proving what you have

The most commonly recommended tool for two-factor authentication is the Google Authenticator[161] app.[162] It works like this:

- You install the Google Authenticator app on your smartphone.
- You "associate" Authenticator with your online account. This is usually done by scanning a QR code provided by the set-up process for that account, or by entering a code that's displayed.

The app now begins displaying a six-digit random number that changes every 30 seconds.

---

[160] Resulting in three-factor authentication. This is one of the reasons you'll also see this enhanced security referred to as "multi-factor", to cover the possible combinations.
[161] https://go.askleo.com/googleauthenticator
[162] Or the compatible app Authy. Authy can be installed on multiple devices, allowing any to be used as your second factor.

In reality, the number isn't random at all—it's a complex function of encryption keys created as part of the process you just completed. It's completely unique to your account and your smart phone. Only the app, and the service you've connected to, know what the number should be at any point in time.

If you can type in the correct number provided by the app when requested by the service, that proves you have that specific smartphone.

Your two factors are:
- *Something you know*: the password to your account, which you prove you know by typing it in as usual.
- *Something you have*: your phone, which you prove you have by entering the number displayed by the Authenticator app when requested.

Your log-in process now requires you to provide your password, and then provide the random number currently being displayed by your smart phone. *Either one by itself is not enough.*

Using SMS for two-factor

An alternative (for those who don't have a smartphone or who just prefer it) is to use text messaging (SMS) to prove you have your phone.

Set up is simple: you give your mobile number to the service, and tell them you want to use it for two-factor authentication.

Your two factors are:
- *Something you know*: the password to your account, which you prove you know by typing it in as usual.
- *Something you have*: your phone, which you prove you have by entering the number text-messaged to it when you try to log in.

Your log-in process now requires you to provide your password and the number texted to your phone.

Some systems can use automated voice readout of the number, meaning you don't need to use texting at all; you don't even need to have a mobile phone — a landline will do. When you try to log in, a voice call is made to your phone number and an automated system reads you the number you need to type in.

While there are occasional stories of SMS being hacked, the reality is that using SMS two-factor is still much more secure than not using two-factor at all.[163]

---

[163] https://askleo.com/70786

Making two-factor less annoying

Once people understand two-factor, the first reaction is usually a horrified, "You mean I have to do this every time I log in?"

Nope.

After you log in *once* using two-factor authentication, most services let you limit how often the second factor will be required on that device. You usually have the following options:

- *Never again on this computer*. This means that this computer itself is trusted. You can log in again on this specific computer without requiring the second factor. (Clearing cookies usually resets this per browser session.)
- *Every-so-often on this computer.* This usually means the service will not ask for a second factor again for some number of days—often 30. (Clearing cookies will reset this, too.)
- *Always ask*. Two-factor authentication is always required.

This lets you tailor exactly how aggressive two-factor authentication should be.

On a computer at home, you might never use two-factor, but on a mobile device or laptop you travel with, you might require it always be used in case you lose the laptop. This is exactly what I do.

Two-factor protects even if you enable and never use it

"Why would I choose 'never ask again'?"

"Never ask again" can apply only to a computer on which you've successfully used two-factor *at least once*. On any computer you've never used, two-factor will always be required at least once.

That means the computer of a hacker who has stolen your password can't be used to get in.

This is how two-factor authentication keeps you secure: *Even if they know your password, hackers cannot log in if you have two-factor authentication enabled.*

Losing your second factor

"What happens if I lose my phone?" (Or other two-factor device).

When you set up your account with something like Google Authenticator, you will also be given a set of *one-time passwords* or recovery codes. *Save those someplace secure.* You can log in with each of those passwords exactly once without requiring your second factor.

Usually you would:

- Log in using a one-time password.
- Temporarily disable two-factor authentication.
- Change the password for safety (optional, but recommended).
- Re-enable two-factor authentication, associating a new phone or other two-factor device.

I save the one-time passwords in an encrypted file.[164]

Some services, like Microsoft, will also let you set up a recovery code[165] that's independent of two-factor authentication. I recommend you do so.

If you're using SMS as your two-factor mechanism, recovery can be as simple as going to your mobile provider and getting a replacement phone while keeping your mobile number. Texts are sent to your mobile *number*, and will follow you to whatever phone you switch to.

Two-factor availability

I have two-factor authentication enabled on everything that supports it. For me, that means, among other things, my bank, Amazon, Gmail, LastPass, Dropbox, Facebook, Evernote, Microsoft, TeamViewer, and even my World of Warcraft account.

Unfortunately, not every service supports two-factor authentication. I strongly recommend you consider it for those accounts that do.

You'll also find that in addition to, or instead of, the two common methods I mentioned above—Google Authenticator and text messaging—several services also have other approaches to two-factor. Facebook allows you to use the Facebook mobile app to provide the code. Some services provide keychain fobs that display the randomly changing number. Other services use devices like the USB-based YubiKey.

Pick what makes the most sense to you, but add two-factor authentication to increase the security of your most important accounts, if not all of them.

---

[164] This is an excellent use, for example, of the secure note feature in many password managers — with the exception of the one-time codes for the password manager itself, of course.
[165] https://askleo.com/16142

The Easy-to-Avoid Two-Factor Loss Risk

I'm a big believer in using two-factor authentication for online accounts.

Two-factor authentication (often referred to as multi-factor authentication, 2FA, or MFA) adds the requirement of "something you have" to "something you know" to log in to an online service.

The risk is that "something you have" could turn into "something you've lost". If you need it and don't have it, you might not be able to sign in.

The solution? Preparation.

Two-factor and "something you have"

You're already familiar with "something you know" — that's a password.

Something you *have* might be a mobile phone capable of receiving a text message, an authenticator app on a mobile device, a dedicated key fob, or even a specialized USB device. Two-factor authentication simply means that you must provide not only a password but proof that you possess a second factor. If you don't, you can't sign in, *even if you know the password.*

Neither can hackers — and that's the point.

The scenario: losing "something you have"

It's one of the first questions to come up when I talk about two-factor authentication: what happens if I lose my second factor?

It's a valid concern.

In my case, for example, I have several accounts requiring my mobile phone in order to sign in. I can't tell you the number of times I've attempted to log in on my family-room laptop[166] only to have to go back to my office and get my phone.

What if I didn't have my phone, or it was broken?

What if I were traveling and I lost my phone?

This scenario is something two-factor authentication designers realized would be an issue from the beginning. The result? Recovery codes.

---

[166] Since this is my traveling laptop, I leave security at its highest setting, requiring that second factor for every sign-in.

Two-factor recovery codes

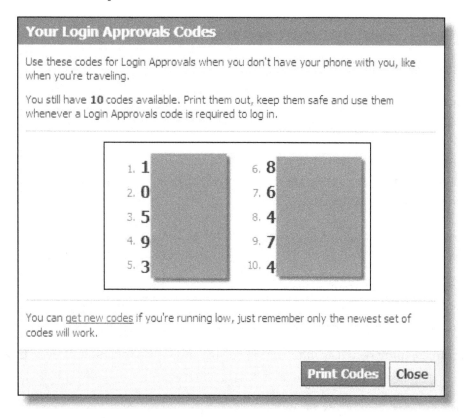

When you set up two-factor authentication, you're also provided with, or prompted to create, recovery information. They typically include options such as:
- Recovery codes: complex codes you can use to sign in without the second factor present.
- One-time passwords: one or more passwords you can use exactly once each to sign in without the second factor present.

In addition, mechanisms you've already put in place to recover your account, such as an alternate email address or mobile phone number, are sometimes also used in lieu of two-factor authentication should you lose that "something you have". In a sense, your ability to get messages at that alternate email address or mobile number is also a type of second factor.

Once signed in successfully, the idea is you would then re-establish two-factor authentication with a new replacement device, or turn 2FA off completely until you can.

But wait ... log in without the second factor? Doesn't that negate the security offered by two-factor authentication?

Not at all.

Keeping recovery codes secure

Remember, you only need recovery codes if you lose your second factor. The rest of the time, they're completely unnecessary.

I have yet to need one of my recovery codes.

The issue, of course, is these recovery codes are like a magic key to get into your account. If anyone besides you could get them, they could get into your account.

That's why it's critical to keep them secure.

Suggestions include:
- Print the codes and keep the print-outs in a safe location, such as a personal safe or safety deposit box.
- Save them digitally to a known and extremely secure location, like your password vault.
- Save them digitally, encrypting the file(s) with tools like 7-zip, BoxCryptor, or others, and then back them up appropriately.

Needless to say, I use the last option. My recovery codes are encrypted and backed up in such a way that I would be able to recover them no matter where I am — even when traveling.[167]

Similarly, keeping your other account recovery information accessible and up-to-date is critical as well. You'll need it if you ever need to regain access to your account, including possibly because you don't have your second factor available.

But as it turns out, keeping recovery information secure and/or up to date isn't even the biggest issue.

Keeping recovery codes at all!

Too many people fail to save the recovery codes at all. Or they forget where they put them. Or they let their alternate email address fall out of use. Or they got a new mobile number and don't update it in their recovery information.

You can guess what happens when they lose their second factor without any way to recover: they lose their account. It's gone, completely, permanently, and without recourse.

When you add a second authentication factor, the advice is simple: don't lose the recovery codes. Keep them secure, and remember where you kept 'em. And of course, keep your other account recovery information up to date as well.[168]

Do that, and you'll have all the security of two-factor authentication without inadvertently locking yourself out should you lose your phone, fob, USB device, or other second factor.

---

[167] In theory. In complete honesty, I've never had to test this scenario, and I hope I never have to. 😊
[168] https://askleo.com/15584

One Way to Lose Your Account Forever

Not a day goes by that I don't hear from someone who's in the middle of some kind of account recovery process that isn't working.

While I try to help out to the degree that I can—usually with instructions that are often no more than the service provider's instructions translated into clearer English— it's also not at all uncommon for those account recovery efforts to fail, and access to the account never be regained.

Never.

And to be super blunt about it, most of the time, it's the account owner's own fault.

The most common reason account recovery fails

Almost every online service has provisions for recovering lost passwords, or recovering access to accounts that are in some way inaccessible to their rightful owners. Those account recovery processes typically involve sending an email to an email address, or a text message to a phone, or something else.

Those are great, reliable approaches to proving you are the rightful owner of the account and should be allowed back in. Anything less would allow hackers to impersonate or otherwise scam the system to break into accounts where they have no business being.

The problem?

Many people don't set up this recovery information, and those that do often don't keep their information current.

Without it, there's almost no hope for recovery.

Alternate email addresses

You should never, ever, have just a single email address these days.

You need at least two.

One you consider to be your real or primary address. The second can be configured as your "alternate" email address for that primary account. It is used should you ever need to prove that you are you ...

... like, perhaps, when you forget your password ...

... or when your account is hacked.

How do you prove that you are you? By being able to access that second email account. Account recovery frequently

involves sending a password-reset link, or a code, or some other kind of information to that other email address, which proves you have access to that account. Since you're the one who set it up as the alternate account, then you must be who you say you are, and thus should be allowed back into the account.

Never set up an alternate email address? You can't recover.

Lost access to the alternate email account? You can't recover.

The conundrum of the phone

Many services now allow you to associate a phone number with your account.

Unduly paranoid folks believe this amounts to more ways for the service in question to keep tabs on them.

Needless to say, I disagree.

Phone numbers are another way to prove you are who you are. Rather than sending you an email, these services can opt instead to send you a text message with a recovery code, or in some cases, a recorded voice to read that recovery code to you. Your ability to receive a code at the phone number you provided proves that you must be you, and once again should be allowed back into the account.

The conundrum I allude to is twofold:
- Many services only support text messaging, and thus mobile phones. You'll need to use a different alternative authentication mechanism—like that alternate email account—if you don't have a mobile phone.
- This typically fails if you lose access to your account, or are asked for additional validation, while traveling outside your own country. Once again, make sure you have an alternate identification mechanism in place—like that alternate email address—before you leave.

Nonetheless, I do advise setting this up if you can.

Losing your account in one easy step

Pick whichever approach you like:
- Don't set up alternate authentication mechanisms like alternate email addresses or phone numbers at all.

Or
- Let your alternate authentication mechanisms expire, change, or lose access to them without updating the account for which they're the alternate mechanism.

Either works. You'll lose access to your primary account *forever* if you ever get hacked or lose your password.

Do this NOW

To avoid losing access to your important accounts, I strongly recommend that you:

- Set up an alternate authentication mechanism on your important accounts.
- If you already have, go check they're all still valid.

I also recommend that you take advantage of all the alternate mechanisms offered.

- Set up an alternate email address, and keep that alternate email address active.
- Set up more than one alternate email address if you can.
- Associate a mobile phone number with the account.
- If you don't have a mobile, and the service will do voice calls (reading you a recovery code) then associate a landline number with the account.

And above all, any time any of the above changes, make absolutely certain to *update the information* in your accounts. Alternate email addresses or phone numbers do you no good if you no longer have access to them.

Email Hacked? Seven Things You Need to Do Now

It seems like not a day goes by when I don't get a question from someone that boils down to their email account having been hacked.

Someone, somewhere, has gained access to their account and is using it to send spam, access other online accounts, hassle contacts, and more. Sometimes passwords are changed, sometimes not. Sometimes traces are left, sometimes not. Sometimes everything in the account is erased—including contacts and saved email—and sometimes not.

If that's happening to you, your email account has been hacked.

Here's what to do next if it happens to you.

1. Recover your account

Log in to your email account via your provider's website.

If you can log in successfully, consider yourself *extremely* lucky, and proceed to Step 2 right away.

If you can't log in, even though you're sure you're using the right password,[169] then the hacker has probably changed your password. *The password you know is no longer the correct password.*

You must then use the "I forgot my password" or other account recovery options offered by the service.

This usually means the service will send password-reset instructions to an alternate email address that you do have access to, or send a text message to a mobile phone number set up previously.

If the recovery methods don't work—because the hacker changed everything, or because you no longer have access to the old alternate email or phone—then you may be out of luck.[170]

If recovery options don't work for whatever reason, your only recourse is to use the customer service phone numbers or email addresses provided by that email service. For free email accounts, *there is usually* no *customer service*. Your options are generally limited to self-service recovery forms, knowledge base articles, and official discussion forums where service representatives may (or may not) participate. For paid accounts, there are typically additional customer service options that are more likely to be able to help.

---

[169] https://askleo.com/15079
[170] https://askleo.com/15584

Important: If you cannot recover access to your account, *it is now someone else's account*. I can't stress this enough. It is now the hacker's account. Unless you've backed up, everything in it is gone forever, and you can skip to Step 5. You'll need to set up a new account from scratch and start over.

2. Change your password

Once you regain access to your account (or if you never lost it), *immediately* change your password.

As always, make sure that it's a good password:[171] easy to remember, difficult to guess, and long. In fact, the longer the better,[172] but make sure your new password is at least 16 characters or more— ideally 12 or more, if the service supports it. See How Long Should a Password Be? for more information.

But don't stop there.

Changing your password is not enough.[173]

3. Change your recovery information

While a hacker has access to your account, they might leave your password alone so that you won't notice the hack for a while longer.

But whether they change your password or not, they may change *all of the recovery information.*

The reason is simple: when you finally do change your password, the hacker can follow the "I forgot my password" steps and *reset the password out from underneath you,* using the recovery information they set.

Thus, you need to check all of it and change much of it ... right away.

- **Change the answers to your secret questions**. They don't have to match the questions (you might say your mother's maiden name is "Microsoft"); all that matters is that the answers you give during a future account recovery match the answers you set here today.
- **Check the alternate email address**(es associated with your account, and remove any you don't recognize. The hacker could have added his or her own. Make sure you have alternate email addresses configured, and that they are accounts that belong to you that you can access. I really can't emphasize that last point enough: the number of accounts that are lost because the recovery email address could no longer be accessed is amazing.
- **Check any phone numbers** associated with the account. The hacker could have set their own. Remove any you don't recognize. Make sure that if you do provide a phone number, it's yours and no one else's, and you have access to it. As with alternate email addresses, I really can't emphasize the last point enough: the number of accounts that are lost because the recovery mobile number could no longer be accessed is scary.

---

[171] https://askleo.com/5440
[172] https://askleo.com/4844
[173] https://askleo.com/15053

These are the major items, but some email services have additional information they use for account recovery. Take the time *now* to research what that information might be. If it's something a hacker could have altered, change it to something else appropriate for you.

Overlooking information used for account recovery allows the hacker to easily hack back in. Make sure you take the time to carefully check and reset all as appropriate.

It's a simple trap too many people fall into causing them to lose their email account forever. Check out A One-step Way to Lose Your Account ... Forever.[174]

4. Check "out of office" messages, reply-to, forwards, and signatures

If your email service provides an out-of-office or vacation-autoresponder feature, or some kind of automatic signature that appears at the bottom of every email you send, it's possible people already know you're hacked.

Hackers often set an auto-responder in a hacked account to automatically reply with their spam. Each time someone emails you, they get this fake message in return, often written so it sounds like you sent it.

If your account includes the ability to set a different "Reply-To:" email address, make sure that hasn't been set. Hackers can set this so individuals who think they're replying to you end up replying to the hacker instead.

Make sure your email is not being automatically forwarded to another email address. If it's available, hackers often set this option to receive copies of every email you get. They can use this to break into your account again, even after you recover it.

Check any signature feature the service supports. Hackers often set up a signature so that every email you send includes whatever they're promoting, including a link to a malicious web site.

5. Check related accounts

This is perhaps the scariest and most time-consuming aspect of account recovery. The risks are high, so understanding this is important.

While the hacker has access to your account, they have access to your email, including past and current emails as well as what arrives in the future.

Let's say the hacker sees you have a notification email from your Facebook account. The hacker now knows you have a Facebook account, and the email address you use for it. The hacker can go to Facebook, enter your email address, and request a password reset.

A password reset sent to your email account—which the hacker has access to.

---

[174] https://askleo.com/15584

As a result, the hacker can now hack your Facebook account by virtue of having hacked your email account.

In fact, the hacker can now gain access to any account associated with the hacked email account.

Like your bank. Or PayPal.

Let me say that again: *because the hacker has access to your email account, he or she can request a password reset be sent to it* from any other account for which you use this email address. In doing so, the hacker can hack and gain access to those accounts.

What you need to do: check your other accounts for password resets you did not initiate and any other suspicious activity.

If there's any doubt, consider changing the passwords on all those accounts as well. (There's a very strong argument for checking or changing the recovery information for these accounts, just as you checked on your email account, for all the same reasons.)

6. Let your contacts know

Some disagree with me, but I recommend letting your contacts know that your account was hacked, either from the account once you've recovered it, or from your new email account.

Inform all the contacts in the online account's address book; that's the address book the hacker had access to.

I believe it's important to notify your contacts so they know not to pay attention to email sent while the account was hacked. Occasionally, hackers try to impersonate you to extort money from your contacts. The sooner you let them know the account was hacked, the sooner they'll know that any such request—or even the more traditional spam that might have come from your account—is bogus.

7. Start backing up

A common reaction to my recommendation that you let your contacts know is: "But my contacts are gone! The hacker erased them all, and all of my email as well!"

Yep. That happens.

It's often part of a hacker not wanting to leave a trail—they delete everything they've done, along with everything you have. Or had.

If you're like most people, you've not been backing up your online email. All I can suggest at this point is to see if your email service will restore it for you. *In general, they will not.* Because the deletion was not their doing, but rather the doing of someone logged into the account, they may simply claim it's your responsibility.

Hard as it is to hear, they're absolutely right.

Start backing up your email now. Start backing up your contacts now.

For email, that can be anything from setting up a PC to periodically download the email, to setting up an automatic forward of all incoming email to a different account, if your provider supports that. For contacts, it could be setting up a remote contact utility (relatively rare, I'm afraid) to mirror your contacts on your PC, or periodically exporting your contacts and downloading them, which is what I do.

8. Learn from the experience

Aside from "you should have been backing up," one of the most important lessons to learn from this experience is to consider all of the ways your account could have been hacked, and then take appropriate steps to protect yourself from a repeat occurrence in the future.

- Use strong passwords that can't be guessed, and don't share them with *anyone*.
- Don't fall for email phishing attempts. If they ask for your password, they are bogus.[175]
- Don't click on links in email that you are not 100% certain of. Many phishing attempts lead you to bogus sites that ask you to log in, and then steal your password when you try.
- If you're using WiFi hotspots, learn to use them safely.[176]
- Keep the operating system and other software on your machine up-to-date, and run up-to-date security software.[177]
- Learn to use the internet safely.[178]
- Consider multi-factor authentication. More and more services support this.

If you are fortunate enough to be able to identify exactly how your password was compromised (it's not common), then absolutely take measures so that it never happens again.

9. If you're not sure, get help

If the steps above seem too daunting or confusing, then definitely get help. Find someone who can help you get out of the situation by working through the steps above.

While you're at it, find someone who can help you set up a more secure system for your email, and advise you on the steps you need to take to prevent this from happening again.

Then follow those steps.

---

[175] https://askleo.com/3863
[176] https://askleo.com/4790
[177] https://askleo.com/3517
[178] https://askleo.com/3517

The reality is that you and I are ultimately responsible for our own security. That means taking the time to learn, and setting things up securely.

Yes, additional security can be seen as an inconvenience. In my opinion, dealing with a hacked email account is *significantly more* inconvenient, and occasionally downright dangerous. It's worth the trouble to do things right.

If that's still too much ... well ... expect your account to get hacked again.

10. Share this article

As I said, email account theft is rampant.

Share this article with friends and family. Statistically, one of you will soon encounter someone whose account has been hacked and will need this information.

Addendum: Is it my computer or not?

When faced with this situation, many people worry that malware on their computer is responsible.

That is *rarely* the case.

In the vast majority of these situations, your computer was never involved.

The problem is not on your computer. The problem is simply that someone else knows your password and has logged into your account. They could be on the other side of the planet, far from you and your computer (and often, they are).

Yes, it's possible that a keylogger was used to capture your password. Yes, it's possible that your PC was used improperly at an open WiFi hotspot. So, yes, absolutely, scan it for malware and use it safely, but don't think for a moment that once you're malware free, you've resolved the problem. *You have not.*

You need to follow the steps outlined here to regain access to your account and protect it from further compromise.

You'll use your computer, but your computer is not the problem.

Part 6: Protect Your Privacy

You're Just Not That Interesting (Except When You Are): Pragmatic Privacy

Privacy is a huge and controversial topic. So huge I can't tell you what steps to take, what settings to change, what apps to avoid, or what services to choose. Not only are there seemingly infinite options, but the options keep changing.

There are also about as many opinions on the topic as there are internet users. Anything I say is just one more voice in the crowd... but that's not going to stop me.

Let's take a pragmatic look at your privacy and your options.

Two kinds of privacy

"Privacy" is a really big term, so I want to define two types:

Implicit privacy is the privacy we assume when we use online services, operating systems, applications, and programs to manage our personal information and activities. Each has a set of rules -- often some formal privacy policy -- controlling their access to your information and what they do with it.

Explicit privacy is the privacy we control more directly with our choices. For example, choosing not to share a photo on social media is one form of explicit privacy. Keeping our passwords to ourselves is another. So are the settings we use to control who is allowed to see what we post.

The biggest difference between implicit and explicit privacy, in my mind, is the amount of control we have over it. We *implicitly* trust that the software and services will do as they say. We *explicitly* decide what to share based on what we believe may happen.

Privacy, policies, and Big Brother

Privacy -- or lack thereof -- when using popular services or software is big topic of discussion. For example, Windows 10's tracking activity generates a great deal of concern. It's debatable whether the concern is warranted.

Any online service involves some amount of tracking. Visiting a simple website—even Ask Leo!— results in some amount of what might be considered "tracking", usually in relation to advertising displayed on the site. Some consider that an invasion of privacy. The most common visible signs are advertisements appearing to follow you[179] from site to site as you browse the web.

All online services and websites have the ability to collect vast amounts of data derived from their users. Similarly, any and all software you install has the ability to collect usage information.

---

[179] https://askleo.com/5670

Whether or not you believe Big Brother is watching, the technology is there should he want to.

The (poor) choices we make

At the other end of the privacy spectrum are the (often poor) choices we make about what we share and with whom.

I often hear from individuals who've shared a password with a trusted friend, only to be surprised when their privacy is violated because the trust was misplaced.

We've all heard stories of individuals losing jobs or job opportunities because of statements, photos, or videos posted on social media. Call your boss names on Twitter, for example, and there's no one to blame but yourself when you're shown the door the next morning. Have you posted "funny" pictures of yourself after imbibing a tad too much alcohol? That could be the reason you don't get the next job or loan you apply for.

When it comes to privacy, we're often our own worst enemy.

You're just not that interesting

I say it often: you and I just aren't that interesting as individuals. That your operating system might track what you do is pretty meaningless in terms of personal privacy. That advertisers might use what websites you visit and things you click on to tailor the ads you see is pretty benign.

The companies collecting this data aren't looking at you as an individual. They're looking for trends from the data of millions of users to determine what's being acted on, what's influencing the crowd, and what they might do better.

I do it, too. For example, do I care that you, specifically, looked at my newsletter? At a personal level I do, but I'm not going to sift through information on nearly 50,000 subscribers to see who did and who didn't. On the other hand, if 10,000 fewer people open the newsletter one week, that's information I want to be able to act on. I can only do that by tracking the behavior of 50,000 individuals in aggregate.

The same is true for most any company. Your personal privacy isn't being violated because nobody is looking at you specifically. One person just isn't that interesting; thousands or millions, on the other hand, almost certainly are.

But you might be interesting someday

There are two cases in which you might become "interesting".

If you run afoul of the law. This isn't an issue for most. But if you live in an oppressive regime or are subject to investigation for your activities, it could be. Even this falls into two sub-categories: the unduly paranoid (a larger number of people than we might hope), and the legitimately concerned, for both legal and illegal reasons.

It is important to realize that if you fall into this category, law enforcement may have the right to collect information about you. This can include things we might brush off as irrelevant — like ad or service usage collected by your ISP, or the services and software you use. I have to say law enforcement may have the right, because laws differ dramatically depending on where you live. Of more practical import, perhaps, law enforcement capabilities vary dramatically, based on everything from expertise to budget to jurisdiction to prioritization of limited resources.

Future opportunities. Some years from now, perhaps someone will research your history as part of a job application or something else where your record and reputation are important. What you post today, publicly or even privately, may influence their opinion tomorrow.

It's all so scary. What to do?

It'd be easy to read that last section, throw up your hands, and crawl into a hole, thinking privacy is a thing of the past -- at least when it comes to the internet.

If you're a criminal, you probably should be concerned. The only thing preventing you from being exposed is the limited resources of the law enforcement agencies who really do care about you specifically. There are steps you can take, but I'm not the one to help you take them.

For the rest of us living more mundane lives, my advice is pretty simple.

First, stop worrying about being tracked by the companies providing the services you use. They don't care about you as an individual. There is plenty of room for policy debate about what kinds of information they should and should not collect and how they should or should not use it, but in my opinion, that has little chance of impacting you *as an individual.*[180]

Second, don't post anything you wouldn't want made public. Learn the privacy policies and settings of your social media and other applications, and change them and/or change your behavior accordingly. Public once is public forever; there's no calling it back from the internet.

Think twice about what you post privately as well, since you're assuming your private audience won't someday make it public without your approval. This includes social media, but also things you share in any form, be it email, text messaging, or other media. We've all seen situations where communications once thought private were made public to great embarrassment or worse.

Privacy remains your responsibility

I remain a strong believer in our wonderfully interconnected world and all the opportunities it presents.

Naturally, it brings risk as well as reward.

Ultimately, it's *our* responsibility to be aware of those risks, educate ourselves about the possibilities as well as the practical realities, and make careful choices accordingly.

---

[180] And if you're going to worry, then be more consistent. It's funny to me to get rants about the alleged privacy violations of company G, sent via an email address provided by company M, whose activity is on par with G. If the behaviors of the major service providers concern you that much, I know of no solution other than walking away from the internet entirely.

Setting up Windows 10 for Privacy

Since its introduction, Windows 10 has come under a fair amount of heat for various privacy issues.

Depending on what you read and what's been uncovered, it does appear that not all the privacy-related issues are necessarily in your control.

However, much of it is, and much of it begins when you install or update Windows 10.

Using or not using a Microsoft account

We'll start in the setup process at the point where you're asked to add an account.

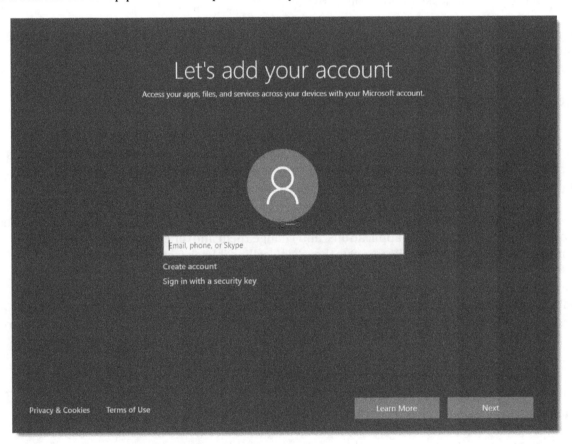

The email address and password you provide are that of your Microsoft account, if you have one. You're also given the opportunity to create one if you don't.

There are pros and cons to using a Microsoft account.

Pros:
- This will become the login for your machine, and it will be associated with your online account.
- Certain features, like Cortana, OneDrive, and the Microsoft Store require the use of your Microsoft account.

- You'll be able to change your login credentials—like your password—without actually needing access to your machine.

Cons:

- You may be sharing even more information with Microsoft about how and where you use your computer.
- It may be another online account to manage if you don't already have one.

Needless to say, many are concerned and choose to operate without a Microsoft account. I don't recommend this. I believe it is important to have a Microsoft account associated with the machine. If you want to use a local machine account for day-to-day use, I recommend setting that up separately, after Windows 10 setup has completed.

After entering your Microsoft account email address and successfully signing in to the account, Windows Setup will suggest you create a PIN to sign in.

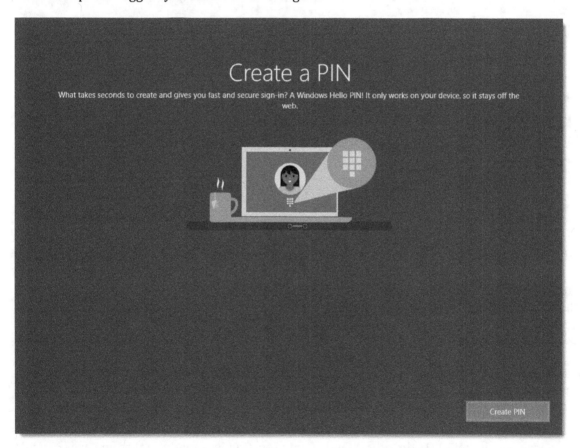

I recommend using a PIN as it's typically easier to sign in with, and just as secure.[181]

---

[181] https://askleo.com/24089

Privacy options

You're then presented with a screen full of privacy options.

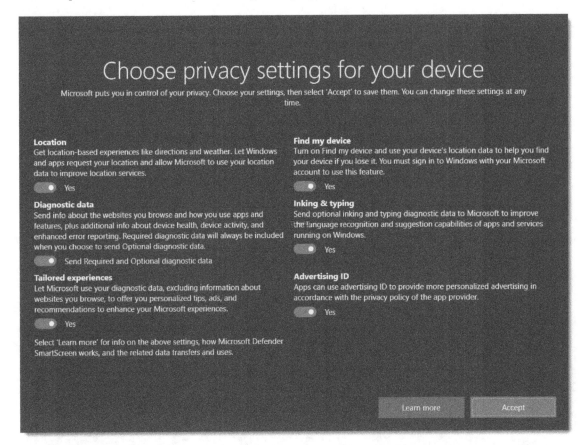

Naturally, the default is to share as much with Microsoft as possible.

My most important recommendation is simply to not blindly click "Accept", but rather examine each privacy setting to make an informed decision.

The settings and my recommendations:

Location: Get location-based experiences like directions and weather. Let Windows and apps request your location and allow Microsoft to use your location data to improve location services.

- Yes. This often enables additional features and functionality in apps and websites that request it. (You can later control whether this information is shared with specific websites as you visit them.) On the other hand, if your location is something that you are particularly concerned about, perhaps you'll feel more comfortable with "No", and living with the resulting loss of features.

Diagnostic data: Send info about the websites you browse and how you use apps and features, plus additional info about device health, device activity, and enhanced error reporting. Required diagnostic data will always be included when you choose to send Optional diagnostic data.

- Yes. Windows will collect information about the websites you browse and how you use apps and features. Microsoft claims that data is anonymized and collected in a non-personally-identifiable way. I believe this information is used for future product enhancements. Of course, if you don't trust Microsoft, this would be one to turn off. If you say No, you'll be presented with an item to "Send required diagnostic data," which I believe is required and used when programs fail or crash.

Tailored experiences: Let Microsoft use your diagnostic data, excluding information about websites you browse, to offer you personalized tips, ads, and recommendations to enhance your Microsoft experiences.

- No. This allows Microsoft to use the data collected in the previous item to make suggestions and target advertisements. It's won't affect how you use Windows. Also, I tend to generally be anti-tip myself, not finding them particularly useful.

Find my device: Turn on Find my Device and use your device's location data to help you find your device if you lose it. You must sign in to Windows with your Microsoft account to use this feature.

- Yes. If you have location turned on, I recommend turning this on as well, if you have a portable device.

Inking & typing: Send optional inking and typing diagnostic data to Microsoft to improve the language recognition and suggestion capabilities of apps and services running on Windows.

- No. You may not want what you've typed or written to be sent to Microsoft. Presumably, this also eats up additional bandwidth. Since this appears to really only be used for future product improvement, there's no real reason to turn it on.

Advertising ID: Apps can use advertising ID to provide more personalized advertising in accordance with the privacy policy of the app provider.

- No. Unless you like "more personalized advertising", I think we're all pretty tired of it.

After you've made the appropriate selections, click Accept to move on.

Privacy matters

The privacy issues around Windows 10 are as important as they are murky.

On one hand, these are often issues that we regularly accept on other platforms, with other companies, and using other technologies, without so much as a second thought. It's very possible -- likely, even -- that the information collected here really is used to improve our experience with Windows, as well as to make it a better operating system for everyone.

On the other hand, in Windows 10 Microsoft seems to be taking information-gathering to a level never before seen in their flagship product, while also being perceived as less than transparent about what is collected, whether we opt-out or not.

Regardless of the outcome, it's important to be aware of the choices made available, even if they're not the default, and make our own decisions.

Facebook Privacy Settings

As I've said before, one way privacy issues happen is through people's own actions. Over-sharing on social media is the most common example.

Nowhere is that more common than on Facebook, where privacy settings are so complex it's often difficult to know exactly who can see what, when, and where.

Let's review Facebook's privacy settings, and perhaps most importantly, what they might imply.

But first, a caveat

One of the issues we face with technology is change. Just about the time we have something figured out, it changes for one reason or another.

Experience shows this is particularly true for Facebook. Presumably, to make things clearer and more secure, Facebook occasionally changes the options and settings they provide, as well as how and where they're configured.

It's quite possible that what I show you today may change by the time you read this.

I'll avoid very much "click here, then here" type of instruction, since it is most likely to be invalidated by future changes. Instead, I'll focus more on walking through and discussing each of the current settings.

App versus website

I recommend you make changes to your Facebook account's privacy settings by visiting facebook.com in a web browser on a desktop or laptop PC. I believe that the privacy settings are clearer, easier to find, and more completely defined there than in the app.

I'm sure that most can also be adjusted by using an app on a mobile device, but this is important enough that the additional clarity and ease of access is important.

I'll use facebook.com for the screenshots here.

How do you use Facebook?

Before altering your privacy settings, it's important to ask yourself, "How do I want to use Facebook?"

Do you want to be easy or difficult to find?

Do you want to share everything with the world, or just a few select friends?

How do you define "friend"? Close friends in real life? People you've met? People you've never met but correspond with? People you recognize? Anyone with a pulse?

The answers to each of these questions impact the settings you choose. If you choose the private/close friends route, you might elect to make it difficult to be found and restrict who sees whatever you share. On the other hand, if you're someone using Facebook as part of a public persona, you might choose more public settings.

The choice is up to you. But do make it a choice rather than an accident, particularly since Facebook's defaults tend towards more public access.

Facebook settings

Click the downward-pointing triangle in the upper-right of the Facebook page to expose a drop-down menu of options. On that menu, click Settings & Privacy.

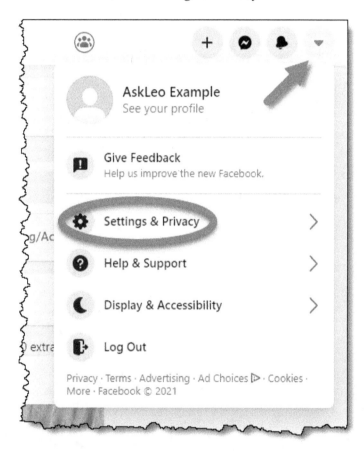

A different drop-down menu will appear. Ignore the "Privacy" items, but click on **Settings**.

This will bring you to the full Facebook settings collection.

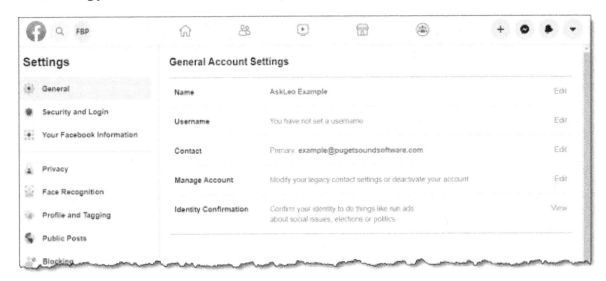

Click on **Privacy** in the left-hand pane.

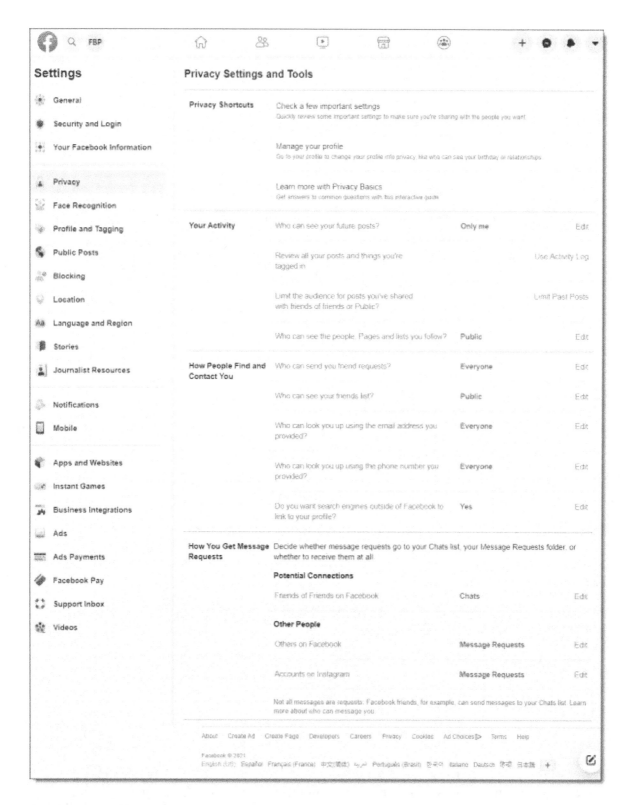

Privacy shortcuts

The upper section contains a few shortcuts: Privacy Checkup, Manage your profile, and Learn More with Privacy Basics.

Privacy Checkup: This will walk you through most of your current settings, and also include security, app access, and advertising settings along the way.

I'll cover individual settings below, but if that seems too overwhelming, at least do this part. You can also return here at any time to review the settings and explanations.

Manage your profile: make changes about what information is displayed in your profile.

Learn more with Privacy Basics: take you to more in-depth information about how to manage your privacy on Facebook.

The rest of the privacy settings are divided into three major areas: Your activity; How people find and contact you; and How you get message requests.

Privacy settings

Your activity

This section is about what happens to the things you put on Facebook, including your posts, comments, tags, and more.

Who can see your future posts? These settings control the visibility of posts you make on Facebook from here on out. Click edit and you'll have access to a drop-down list of the possible options by clicking the downward-pointing triangle next to the current setting.

Two important things to realize about this setting

First, you can change it for each individual post you make, *but it stays at what you last set it to.* So, for example, if you set it to "Friends" here on the settings page, and then set it to "Public" for a specific post you make, *the setting remains "Public" until you change it back.*

Second, restricting access to something less than public, while certainly a reasonable choice, does not prevent those you share it with from further sharing your post in other ways. Nothing prevents them from taking a screenshot of your post and sharing that publicly. You've probably seen screenshots of embarrassing public posts long after the original post has been taken down.

My approach is to leave this setting "Public" at all times and to *remember it's set this way.* This serves as a reminder to me to only post things I'm comfortable with truly being public.

Review all your posts and things you're tagged in is just a shortcut to your Activity Log and Timeline review. This allows you to go back and view (or change) the visibility of your past actions.

Limit the audience for posts you've shared with friends of friends or public? This tool allows you to make wholesale changes to everything you've shared in the past. With it, you can, for example, change all your previously public posts to be restricted to a smaller audience. I've never used this tool, nor would I recommend relying on it. There's just no true way to truly "undo" something done publicly. Your post could have been copied, screen captured, or any number of other things taking it out of your control.

How people find and contact you

Who can send you friend requests? This has two settings: "Everyone" or "Friends of friends". I have this set to "Friends of friends". What you want will depend on how you use Facebook. Fortunately, unwanted friend requests are easy to ignore.

Who can see your friends list? This allows you to assign the same level of privacy as you would a post: Public, Friends, Friends except, and so on. Once again, I have mine set to Public as a reminder that any of my friends who can see the list could copy and share it publicly.

Who can look you up using the email address you provided? Possible settings are "Everyone", "Friends of friends", or just "Friends". I figure if someone knows my personal email address, I don't have a problem with them finding me on Facebook. Again, the setting you choose depends on how you use Facebook.

Who can look you up using the phone number you provided? Possible settings again are "Everyone", "Friends of friends", or just "Friends". My thoughts are similar: if you know my number, it's ok with me that you can find me on Facebook.

Do you want search engines outside of Facebook to link to your profile? Do you want people to be able to find your Facebook profile on Google or Bing or other search engines?

Leo A. Notenboom | Facebook

https://www.facebook.com/leonot

Leo A. Notenboom (N7LEO) is on Facebook. To connect with Leo, sign up for Facebook today.

Occupation: Chief Question Answerer

How you get message requests

This is all about Facebook Messenger and how messages from people who are not a Facebook Friend should appear.

Potential Connections: You can opt to allow friends-of-friends to contact you directly in chat, or in the separate "Message Requests" area without notification, or you can specify that they be discarded.

Other People: You can indicate that Facebook and Instagram messages be sent to the "Message Requests" area or discarded.

Facebook Privacy Basics

Finally, as you may have noticed in the menu we started with, there's currently an item called Privacy Basics at the bottom.

I recommend you take some time to review the information presented there.

If nothing else, the very wording of the Facebook mission is worth noting: "... make the world more open and connected." To me, this indicates their rationale behind making your default settings as open, public, and permissive as they are.

Endnotes

Afterword

I hope this book helps you protect yourself against all the nasty things that happen to you in our internet-connected world.

If you find what you believe to be an error in this book, please register your book (the details are in an upcoming section) and then visit the errata page for this book. That page will list all known errors and corrections, and give you a place to report anything you've found that isn't already listed.

Register Your Book!

I've got additional updates, errata, and other bonus materials for you:

- *Updates For Life* to this book, as they're released.
- Downloads of this book in any or all of three digital formats:
    - PDF (for your computer or any device that can view PDF files)
    - .mobi (ideal for the Amazon Kindle), or
    - .epub (for a variety of other electronic reading devices).
- Other bonuses and supplementary material I might make available in the future.

Registering gives you access to it all.

Visit https://go.askleo.com/regisexpanded *right now* and register.

That link is mentioned *only here,* and it's totally FREE to owners of this book.

About the Author

I've been writing software in various forms since 1976. In over 18 years at Microsoft, I held both managerial and programming roles in a number of groups, ranging from programming languages to Windows Help, Microsoft Money, and Expedia. Since 2003, I've been answering tech questions at the extremely popular *Ask Leo!* website (https://askleo.com) and in other entrepreneurial projects like this book.

Curious for more? Someone asked, and I answered on the site: Who is Leo? (https://askleo.com/who-is-leo/)

Feedback, Questions, and Contacting Leo

I'd love to hear from you.

Honest.

I truly appreciate reader input, comments, feedback, corrections, and opinions—even when the opinions differ from my own!

Here's how best to contact me:
- If you have a comment or a question about this book, I strongly encourage you to register your book, as outlined in above, and use the prioritized comment form in the registered owner's center.
- If you prefer not to register your book, you can email me at leo@askleo.com.
- If you have a computer or tech-related question, the best approach by far is to first search *Ask Leo!* (https://askleo.com). Many, many questions are already answered right there, and finding those answers is much faster than waiting for me.
- If you can't find your answer using Search, visit https://askleo.com/book and submit your question. That's a special form just for book purchasers and it gets prioritized attention.
- If you just want to drop me a line, or have something you want to share that isn't covered above, you can use https://askleo.com/book, or email leo@askleo.com.
- If you're just not sure what to do … email leo@askleo.com. ☺

Copyright and Administrivia

This publication is protected under the U.S. Copyright Act of 1974 and all other applicable international, federal, state, and local laws. All rights are reserved.

Please note that much of this publication is based on my own personal experience and anecdotal evidence. Although I've made every reasonable attempt to achieve complete accuracy of the content in this book, I assume no responsibility for errors or omissions. You should use this information as you see fit and at your own risk.

Any trademarks, service marks, product names, or named features are assumed to be the property of their respective owners. They are used only for reference. Unless specifically stated otherwise, use of such terms implies no endorsement.

Sharing this Document

The bottom line is that you shouldn't.

More specifically, you shouldn't make copies and give them to others.

Loan your copy as you see fit. (Back it up, of course!) However, making an additional copy to *give* to someone else is a no-no. (The rule is pretty simple: if you *loan* the book, they have access to it, and you shouldn't, until they return it. If both you and your friend can use the book at the same time, then you've made a *copy*, and that's the part that's wrong.) That also applies to uploading a copy to an electronic bulletin board, website, file sharing, or similar type of service.

The information in this document is copyrighted. That means giving copies to others is actually *illegal*. But more important than that, it's simply wrong.

Instead, if you think it's valuable enough to share, encourage your friends who need this book to buy a copy of their own. Or, heck, buy one as a gift for them.

Remember, it's the sale of valuable information in books like this one that makes Ask Leo! possible. It's pretty simple, really; if enough people disregard that, there'd be no more books, and eventually no more Ask Leo!

There is also a FREE edition of *The Ask Leo! Guide to Staying Safe On the Internet* which may be shared with others. Register your copy of *this* book, as described in a prior chapter, and you'll have access to that one as well.

More Ask Leo! Books

If you found this book helpful, check out my library of books at https://askleo.com/shop.

www.ingramcontent.com/pod-product-compliance
Lightning Source LLC
LaVergne TN
LVHW060122070326
832902LV00019B/3087